I06.33467

Wakefield Press

ACCIDENTAL GARDENS

Rob Carney grew up in Washington state in the Pacific Northwest but moved to Salt Lake City, Utah in 1997. He is the author of nine books of poems, including *The Book of Drought* (Texas Review Press 2024), which won the X.J. Kennedy Poetry Prize. He has received the Milton Kessler Memorial Prize and the Robinson Jeffers/Tor House Foundation Award for Poetry, and his work has appeared in dozens of journals, as well as in the Norton anthology *Flash Fiction Forward* (2006). He is a Professor of English at Utah Valley University and writes a regular feature called "Old Roads, New Stories" for *Terrain.org*.

PRAISE FOR
ACCIDENTAL GARDENS: NEW & REVISED

With his clarity, directness and humour, Rob Carney writes like Richard Brautigan in an age of ecological collapse. This collection of flash essays and poems is a journey through the absurdity, tragedy and black comedy of late-stage capitalist and consumerist America, weaving between despair and hope like sixty million spawning salmon. It is also a map that points us towards how the damage might be repaired—a reminder to open our eyes and to pay attention.

—Nick Hunt, author of
Where the Wild Winds Are and
Editor at The Dark Mountain Project

ACCIDENTAL GARDENS

New & Revised

Rob Carney

Wakefield
Press

Wakefield Press
16 Rose Street
Mile End
South Australia 5031
www.wakefieldpress.com.au

First published by Stormbird Press 2021
This edition published 2025

Copyright © Rob Carney, 2021, 2025

All rights reserved. This book is copyright. Apart from any fair dealing for the
purposes of private study, research, criticism or review, as permitted under
the Copyright Act, no part may be reproduced without written permission.
Enquiries should be addressed to the publisher.

Supported by a grant from the Government of South Australia.

Edited by Maddy Sexton, Wakefield Press
Text designed and typeset by Jesse Pollard, Wakefield Press

ISBN 978 1 92338 805 5

A catalogue record for this
book is available from the
National Library of Australia

Wakefield Press thanks
Coriole Vineyards for
continued support

For Bama, Ozzly, Quentin,
Jaybird, and Rhyan

CONTENTS

Dear Reader,

When my brother and I were kids, our parents took us to Jamaica. Bananas everywhere. On the cab ride from the airport: bananas, these whole plantations of them just outside the window. At a snarl in the traffic where we had to slow down: someone knocking on the hood, selling bananas. And in the hotel lobby while checking in, a woman asked my dad if he wanted to buy some bananas—she had a whole branch hoisted on her shoulder—but my dad just answered no thank you, and the woman moved on.

Later that night at dinner, in the hotel's courtyard, this couple crossed over from the bar and asked my mom, "Are you guys from the States?"

She said, "We are." She said, "We're from Washington."

"We're from Minneapolis," they told her. "Do yourself a favor and order a banana daiquiri."

"But I don't like banana daiquiris."

"That's okay. Just do it and see what happens." Then they left.

And so my mom did. The waiter came by, and she asked him, but he told her no. The restaurant was out of bananas.

Now flash ahead to today: I'm just off the phone with my phone company. They've gotten my bill wrong again, as if they, too, want me to give up my landline, and sucking is their strategy to finally make that happen (and it worked because I cancelled with them, but that's getting ahead of the story).

Anyway, I do the ten-minute robot menu, do the twenty minutes on hold. Then a woman picks up on the other end and says, "I see that you're calling from yada yada yada; is that correct?"

"It is."

"And are you the primary contact?"

"I am."

"And your full name? Your email for verification? Last four digits of your social? Five things you'd rather be doing right now? Your love of redundancy on a scale of one-to-a-million? Now, what was your question exactly?"

"Not a question," I said, "a statement: You charged me double on my latest bill, plus an $18 late fee."

"A moment, please, while I look up your account. . . Yes, I see. Would you like to pay that balance now?"

"I already did."

"Not according to our records."

"Well, my bank records show that my check for March was cashed and cleared."

Since you've probably lived through this plot line yourself, I'll just skip ahead to the ending:

"Okay, then, I've waived the bill for March. Are there any other questions?"

"What about the late fee?"

"I can waive that too."

"So what's the new total for April?"

"The same as before."

"But you just said—"

"You pay the whole total on your statement now, then we credit you in May."

"But that's ridiculous."

"You don't have a choice."

"Then I want those credits in writing. You can send it to my email."

"No I can't."

"How come?"

"Because we aren't connected to the internet."

"But you're also my internet provi—"

"Listen, I'm not gonna sit here and explain our whole system for you."

"What system?" I asked.

"The way we do things," she said.

"I have an idea," I said. "I think it might be a good one. Is there anyone there I can talk to other than you?"

"Not about this."

"Then can I talk about vintage automobiles? Like the hardtop '56 T-Bird coupe? It's always pictured in Fiesta Red paint, but I prefer the Sunset Coral."

"Yes," she said. "You can talk about that. A supervisor will call you. But first I need your call-back number."

My call-back number?! They're damn the phone company. My number's right there on the statement we've been talking about, the same one they wanted me to verify. It's the whole banana daiquiri again, minus the trip to Jamaica and the courtyard café.

And it's why sometimes I just hang up, disconnect, and try to write instead. Because if the real world can't do better than this, then at least I can imagine a new one.

That's the reason for stories, I think. Or, anyway, it's one of the reasons: In the middle of your daily nonsense, a story swoops over and lands nearby, and all you have to do is notice. You just wait, and listen, and see what happens next.

Among other things (like poetry, place, the environment, and why grizzly bears are accidental gardeners), that's what this book is about. I hope you like it.

Your friend,
Rob Carney

INTRODUCTION TO
ACCIDENTAL GARDENS: NEW & REVISED

BY SIMMONS B. BUNTIN

Yesterday I drove the two hours from my home in Tucson, Arizona, to the Whitewater Draw Wildlife Area, a collection of managed wetlands, trails, and viewing decks a few miles north of the Mexico border. Sandhill cranes by the tens of thousands overwinter here—their graceful necks and gray plumage, their red-capped heads and long black beaks, their raucous, rattling conversations overpowering any other noises except, perhaps, the occasional U.S. Customs and Border Protection Sikorsky helicopter.

Though I had come to experience the vastness of this high-desert landscape and the birds that call it their home, I also felt it important to ask them whether—as our President only days ago declared—there is a national emergency at the border. I had passed two Border Patrol checkpoints on the way down (pulling over only those heading north), as well as Tombstone, home to the most famous shootout in the Old West. I figured the cranes—who have been migrating across North America for at least 2.6 million years—have been around long enough to know an emergency when they see one. Most of their species' timeline, of course, was before the time of nations, but who's to suggest our President doesn't hold the collective wisdom of the eons?

I had planned this February visit between two seminal events: doing my taxes, which I had scheduled for the day after my session with the cranes, and reading Rob Carney's *Accidental Gardens: New & Revised*—this very book you hold now—which I had finished just a few hours before my road trip. My conversation with the Sandhill cranes on that brisk afternoon would serve as an appropriate bridge between the delightful conversation I had been having with Carney in the pages of this book and the conversation with the IRS (well, with the TurboTax bots) I was dreading. Call it

1

my "Stopping by Woods on a Snowy Evening" transition—what I wanted to do versus what I had to do. That the President had opened another line of discourse between me and the cranes with his declaration was unexpected, but fitting.

My consultation with the cranes was, I admit, hit and miss. For one thing, they weren't keen to talk about the President's national emergency along the border when their wisdom spoke to a longer emergency spanning nations and the changing climate of the world. But they recognized that he and his featherless buddies were already doing a lot of damage on public lands—a term a bit ridiculous to the birds, a species older than the hills surrounding Whitewater Draw. (I don't mean to imply the cranes were ill-mannered or had a short span of attention for my questions; rather, they weren't much concerned with the affairs of the day, beyond a slow grasshopper on a reed or the wind quickening out of the west.) Finally, just as I thought I was making headway, the cranes lifted *en masse*—the cerulean sky flush with the silhouettes of these long-winged vases in flight—and I was left in the shower of their riotous calls to answer for myself these other questions of the day.

Which is where Carney and this book come in (or rather, come in again). While the Sandhill cranes of Whitewater Draw weren't much for Q&A, here you'll find that the essays and poems of this collection are not just clever and poetic dialogue—though there is that. Rather, they are a conversation between the author and you, the reader. It's a conversation both whimsical and serious, with tight turns and lines enjambed, with seemingly disconnected elements coming together beautifully. From Halloween to humpback whales to Rainier cherries to Miles Davis—and that's just one essay.

"[A]n imagined town is just as real as an actual town," writes Richard Hugo in *The Triggering Town*. Carney's rich imagination is what seeds these conversations, and from the real challenges of the day—the preservation of public lands, supporting our education system, the salvation of craft in its many important contexts—he spins tales and wisdom from which any creature as far back as the Pliocene would take heart. (I'm looking at you,

Sandhill cranes.) But you too, friend, are that surviving creature—and so are all of us under Carney's delightful, political, philosophical writing.

In a world of alternative truths, Carney gives us the real truth, one only possible through the mind and pen of a poet-essayist. But don't let the author's humility fool you—there is a grand point to the work in this collection, and that is this: Just as the stubbly fields and marshes of Whitewater Draw need the cacophony of crane calls, so we too need voices like Rob Carney's. Like the lead in that long skein of birds on the horizon, they direct us in troubling times and help us decipher emergencies real from emergencies imagined. They humor us, they center us, they free us. Prepare to take flight.

I.

ENVIRONMENTAL STUDIES

ARCHAEOLOGY

Who knew the badgers of Utah were so advanced? Not you. It's no use pretending you did. No, the only people who knew this were Mike Noel and me.

I'll tell you about my own credentials in a minute, but here are his: He was the state representative from Kanab; he was opposed to designating more national monuments; and during interim meetings, he said something interesting. It had to do with the Bears Ears Monument, which is a longer story than I want to catch you up on, but the short version goes like this: Archaeologists by the hundreds sent a petition to then President Obama—they wanted him to designate a Bears Ears monument in order to stop the looting of artifacts—and what Representative Noel (Republican) had to say about it was pretty great. He said, "There is no immediate threat. It's a scam. There's no fresh digging. All we can see today are badger holes. We have got to get a handle on these badgers because those little suckers are going down and digging up artifacts and sticking them in their holes."

Badger antiquities thieves! Oh man. And from the photo evidence collected by the Bureau of Land Management ("F**k you BLM" carved in a rock; bullet holes in a petroglyph), these badgers are fluent in English and carrying guns.

Now, my own credentials aren't political. Me, I just collect odd details, then dust them off and display them the best that I can. My brother Colin, for instance, had some good ones after driving buses in Alaska. He came home awestruck that tourists could be so dumb. When I wondered what he meant by that, he told me some of the things they asked him. Then I went away with a pen and came back with a scrap of brotherly sympathy. I know it's no Grecian Urn, but it made him laugh:

If You Ask a Stupid Question in Alaska. . .

"Is this the same moon I see in Iowa?"

"No."

"Are these the same stars as Illinois?"

"Not quite. See, up here the Big Dipper's a saucepan to simmer the Northern Lights, and the moon above Denali is solid iron. We can pan the air for gold."

"Do polar bears eat people?"

"Not if they're full."

"Well, what about a moose?"

"Of course. Them too. Amazing hunters. Whenever tourists vanish, it's a safe bet a well-fed moose is contentedly asleep."

"Are you pullin' my leg?"

"Do you want to see my scars?"

"So what's the elevation of Anchorage?"

"Probably four. It's right on the water."

"Haha, now I know you're lyin'. We're too far north. . . Hey, what do you call all these trees?"

"We call them the woods. Legends say the bark makes you smarter. Give one a lick."

This Utah badger detail reminds me of that. And it explains so many things succinctly. For instance, there's a high-rise going up where there used to be a toy store. It blocks—which hardly seems possible—our neighborhood view of the Wasatch Mountains. This is just the latest make-over/burial of a once unique area called Sugar House, and throughout this whole construction blitz there's been a moratorium on mitigation funds. Why? Good question, but I'm afraid there isn't a good answer. No, the money that builders normally pay for improvements to parks, road maintenance, and increased fire and police protection to go along with the thousands more residents and cars is instead just money that the builders get to keep. It's been decades since I took Algebra, but the equation looks something like this: Call builders x and long-time residents and businesses

y, where x = \$\$ and y = *@!?*! Yes, it's a lot to put up with, but it helps to know that our former mayor, Ralph Becker, made this decision while hypnotized by badgers.

What else? Badgers have pick-axed common sense and pirated it away. That's why doctors need insurance but gun owners don't. One is in case of malpractice; I get it. But shouldn't we call getting shot malpractice with a gun?

What else? Let's say you're a football fan, and the referees are terrible. Tell me their uniforms don't look a lot like badgers.

What else? Say you can't find joy, or reason, or an adequate, merited pay raise. Grab yourself a flashlight and crawl inside a badger hole. They're probably down there beside some artifacts, clawed a bit but still valuable, brushed off and lined up on badger shelves. Take it from me and Mike Noel.

POLITICAL SCIENCE

One summer the people of Kalispell had too much paint. Driving into town, I saw a car slap-dashed with yellow—must have been two-hundred cartoon lemons—and a homemade signboard bolted on the roof: "Dale's Sales Auto / Lemon Car / No Good." So that was the first example.

The second was this: I was driving a truckload of fireworks to Sandpoint, Bonner's Ferry, Whitefish, etc.; Shelby, Great Falls, and Fort Benton, then back to Spokane, the same loop I'd taken three days before when I went to put up a dozen fireworks stands. So now I'm back in Kalispell, dropping off their order, and they've painted the whole stand with Jesus murals, wow—Son of God with a sparking halo; Messiah with a lamb in one hand, a Roman Candle in the other; one of the Wise Men, Melchior I think, putting Pop-Its in front of the manger—and the Youth Director running things had even more ideas:

"Why don't you sell some Christian fireworks? Instead of these Red Devils. You could add a sticker so people know they're Christian Approved."

"I don't pick the names," I told him. "They make them over in China."

He walked off talking about communists, shaking his head.

Our warehouse was happier, though, calling out test-run firework names, our typically boring and cardboard jobs suddenly not.

"How 'bout the *Star of Bethlehem*."

"And the *Noah Sees a Sunbeam*."

"Or the *30 Pieces of Silver*."

"Or *Let-There-Be-Lights*."

"Maybe the *Cleopatra*?"

"That's not biblical, you idiot."

"I thought she was married to Moses."

"What're you, nuts?"

"What should we call these *Piccolo Petes?*"

"*Little Towers of Babel.*"

"How 'bout the *Cuckoo Fountains?*"

"Just call them *Doves.*"

"Are you sure she didn't marry Moses? I thought I saw it in a movie."

"You think we should re-name the sparklers?"

"No, they're just sparklers. But now with myrrh!"

All of us channeling Byron or something, a bunch of low-wage Shakespeares stopping to sneeze black powder on our sleeves and forgetting about our coffee break; that afternoon flew faster than any of us knew.

But why stop there? Why not specialize for everyone? Aim fireworks at nurses and doctors, cats and dogs. For the dinosaur lover, there's the *Pterodactyl Rocket*. For summer-league baseball teams we've got *Grand Slams*. For the ambidextrous, try these aerials with fuses on both sides. Everything lasered into segments, everything split. Even for surfers—two distinct versions of the *Perfect Wave Fountain*: blue sparks or turquoise, Pacific or South Pacific? Take your pick.

Or yes, we could stick to the same old basics: *United, Indivisible*. Instead of seals of approval, yes, we could just keep fireworks for all.

HOW TO CARVE A PUMPKIN

It's fair to say I write a lot about our built and natural environments. And right now, late October, I can't help thinking that holidays fall into those categories too. We need them instinctively—to mark the change of seasons, wish and give, commemorate and look forward—but we also make them up, creating or inheriting celebrations. Built and natural.

Take Halloween: It isn't generically American, but many people don't know this. It came north out of Mexico, and west with the Irish across the Atlantic; two historically reviled groups—wrong looks, wrong speech, wrong religion—but throw their celebrations in the microwave of marketing, and *presto*: Halloween is mainstream, and everyone's carving jack-o-lanterns.

There's a reason for that, an origin story about where jack-o-lanterns come from. It's about Jack, Ireland's wildest carouser, and it goes like this:

Jack was a bad man, always swearing and brawling. He whirled through women like a lust tornado, pegged rocks at all the cops and priests, so everyone knew that Jack was going to hell.

But Jack was a talker too. He had the gift of persuasion and storytelling. And when the devil came, Jack promised that he could change.

"Just a year's reprieve," he bargained. "I'll quit with my pocket knife and stabbing the asses of my enemies. And these hands won't be for fists anymore but for bringing alms to the nuns on Sunday. And no more getting into underskirts and romping away behind the hedgerows," until finally the devil was impressed and believed him and agreed.

A barrel of lies, of course. Jack went on the same as ever. The year rolled by full of pints and fighting until one night the devil reappeared.

"Mr. Devil," says Jack, "I'm sorry for deceiving you. I'll come along quiet now, I promise. But couldn't I have a last supper before we go? I'm starvin' famished. No? Then how about one last apple, but I'll need you to climb up and reach it for me—that one on the branch near the top should do it—on account of my knuckles are swollen from punching, and my ankle's nearly broken after leaping out a woman's window."

Now, the devil can't believe it, but sure enough he's climbing, shimmying out on a waving branch, when *slash, slash*, there's Jack with his pocket knife, carving a cross in the tree trunk, so now the devil's trapped. He's stuck and ridiculous because he can't get down past that cross, and Jack's away to the pub and waving farewell.

No one can out-talk Death though, and Jack died one day, as we all will. Of course, heaven was as closed as a treasure chest, but it turned out hell was too. The devil never forgave him for his trick that night and sent Jack away into exile in the cold and dark of space. A terrible doom, an endless emptiness, walking and walking through eternity alone.

It was a pretty sad plight, and the devil knew it, so first he gave Jack a bit of hellfire for comfort.

"Get out your clever pocket knife," he said, "and that turnip in your pocket. Carve it out hollow and have yourself this coal, some light for your journeying."

And that's how Jack became Jack of the Lantern.

Of course, Americans have traded in turnips for pumpkins. They're bigger and softer and easier to carve. Most of us don't remember this part, though: Those lanterns are to light the way for the dead to come visit the living, to return each All Hallows Eve and enjoy the food and drink we set out for them. It isn't just custom, it's ceremony.

Trick-or-treating isn't the same, I know. It isn't the best that we can do. But oh well, kids love it, so don't duck out and be gone that night, your house left empty and dark. Stay home and pass out sugar in abundance. In exchange for agreeing to do that, I'll give you these three things in return:

First, humpback whales are amazing. There's a good chance to see them in Monterey Bay. But it's the smell I actually remember most, hanging in the air after they've gone back under, something nostril-searing and ancient, and you can't pass through it like a curtain, a blowhole smell of Ocean-Dead, a smell of considerable size. Second is Rainier cherries. You should definitely eat them. And no, Bings are no substitute. Try to do this in Grandview or Zillah since Mt. Rainier looks different from the east side. Short of that, though, a grocery store will do. Buy pounds, fill up; they're here and gone like orchard lightning. And third is Miles Davis's *My Funny Valentine Live*, his group with George Coleman not Coltrane. Those first haunting notes Miles carves with his trumpet—they'll hollow you out and put a light inside. They're like the prayers that Jack should have offered. . .

May the road rise up to meet you.

Toda la tierra es mi corazón.

Amen.

SOCIAL STUDIES

My kid is 12, and he's reading *Frankenstein*, and he's down to the final ten pages, the part where Victor's giving a speech to Captain Walton's crew—calling them cowards because they want to turn south when the ice breaks—and Quentin groans, "Oh come on, Frankenstein, all you care about is getting to go after your beast." He can read the guy like an X-ray.

Could I have done that when I was 12? I don't know. I was a reader myself, but nothing like this book. In fact, my own clearest memory of seventh grade doesn't have to do with literature at all. It's Mrs. Beulah Felhoffer: Social Studies and Current Events.

The jump in expectations from sixth grade to junior high wasn't the issue. I was diligent and grade-scared. Plus, my dad taught high school Civics, History, Psychology/Sociology, Contemporary World Problems, so I had a ringer in my corner if I needed one. And this was May 19, 1980, the day after Mt. St. Helen's erupted: ash burying all of eastern Washington; the Cowlitz River strangled by wiped-out forests and mud; a man named Harry Truman entombed in his cabin on the shores of Spirit Lake; and even my hometown, Puyallup, which sat north of the ash plume and away from the path of the jet stream, was everywhere dusted in volcano color. Incredible. I brought in the whole damn *News Tribune* and figured it was a slam-dunk A.

I got an F.

My dad was never one of those parents primed to skirmish with anyone who failed to appreciate his offspring, but this time he did ask to meet with my teacher and came home thinking that the woman might really be insane. Apparently she'd told him an acceptable current event was "something important. Like a story on the moon landing." Hers was a rare definition of *current*.

Around this same time, I took an I.Q. test, something my dad was using with his college-prep seniors. Some professor, I guess, had put it together, intending to give White people a jolt. I'd always liked this sort of quizzing. Take Lucky Lager, for instance: If your parents chose Lucky in bottles over cans of Oly or Rainier, it meant you got to solve these puzzles on the inside of the caps; very cool. Anyway, the test had ten or so questions sort of like this:

> Duke Ellington is to piano, as. . .
> a) Billie Holiday is to ballads.
> b) Miles Davis is to trumpet.
> c) Lester Young is to tenor sax.
> d) Dizzy Gillespie is to trumpet.

If you're thinking *You've got to be kidding me,* then you're halfway right. And even if you're thinking that you're hip to this, you're probably still a little unsure, maybe trying to work out the logic: "Do I base my answer on the musical era (Billie Holiday), or on the style (it's swing, so Lester Young), or is it just their names/nicknames beginning with the letter D?" No, no, and no. The only acceptable answer to the question is B. Why?—because Miles, like Duke, was a composer (not Dizzy; he didn't sight read) as well as immortal on trumpet like Ellington was immortal on keys. My test score marked me as illiterate, which didn't feel fair—culturally specific referents aren't basic common knowledge—and that was the point.

And it brings me back to *Frankenstein.* Victor thinks that he's been doomed by Fate, but he's wrong. He's just cocooned in privilege—

> a) Moneyed?
> b) Male?
> c) Racial?
> d) All of the above?

—which isn't the only reason for his ethical near-sightedness, but it doesn't help.

Worse, as Quentin will soon find out while reading the last ten pages, Victor doesn't learn. And if personifying Prideful/Rash Disaster doesn't teach you a clarifying lesson, nothing will.

Two hundred years ago, Mary Shelley knew this. She knew it at the age of 18. I'd rather cast my vote for her than most of the office-seekers these days. Imagine the headline *that* would generate: "Illegal Alien's Ghost Wins Election."

I could mail it to Mrs. Felhoffer and flunk again.

TRIGONOMETRY

I've lived most of my life in Washington and Utah. Throw in all the driving I've done in Oregon, Idaho, Wyoming, and Montana, and it feels like a head start on looking at things. All that size. Everywhere. Iconic and mythic.

And it's myths that actually matter. I can say, "In the Old Songs about Washington, salmon nested in trees," and it isn't untrue. Not in a myth. Not in a story. Not even in fact, it turns out, if you think of tree roots as underground branches, think of nesting as letting go (like sleep, just forever), transforming, becoming nitrogen.

What happens—I learned this a few days ago—is that most of the salmon the bears take from rivers aren't just eaten right there. A lot get carried into the woods, and I love that, love thinking of bears as these clawed and massive accidental gardeners whose table scraps fertilize forests. Trading this for a pipeline down the coast of B.C.'s Inner Channel seems like something only the thoughtless and heart-blind would do. As in, Earth – Bears – Woods = No, no, no. We don't need fewer archetypes and less empathy, we need more. . .

Back when I was in high school, we started at 7:45, which meant starting in blackness during winter. The 49th parallel. The days are short. They start late and end early. My first-period class was Trigonometry, and one time out the back window I saw a thin line of light appear and outline Mt. Rainier. Suddenly there, an orange tracing, a black silhouette.

Another minute and the sun was rising, and this was Washington, overcast, the whole sky ceilinged, so the sun split into streaks of color—pinks and reds and whatever—on the undersides of the clouds. Then things filled in and blended, then the sun was halfway up behind the mountain, and the scene out the window was just another January morning.

I think I got a B+ in Trig that year, or maybe even an A. But those three minutes are the only part I remember.

ADDITION + SUBTRACTION

If there's a Nobel Prize for mountains, it should go to Mt. Rainier. Before I tell you why, though, here's something I learned about Tempe, Arizona. My friend Brian was explaining about buying a house there. "What you do," he said, "is find one you like and then ask the neighbors about scorpions." Some blocks are seething with them, some blocks aren't, and scorpions don't care about poured foundations. Set concrete on ground a thousand scorpions have been calling home and no amount of flooring, framing, and wishing is going to keep them out. Your house will be Scorpion City.

We should remember better than we usually do that details like this are what count. Forget the number of bathrooms, the stainless steel gas range. Go knock on doors along your maybe street and ask, "Scorpions? How many? How many times a day?" Call it the World's Strange Mathematics.

Now, about Mt. Rainier. I know one of the best places to see it: from a leftover scrap of the valley I grew up in. There are two ways to get from Puyallup to Tacoma, Pioneer Way and River Road. One is winding and the other one's straight and, ironically, River Road is the straight one, so usually I'd cut over. Two smaller roads let you do that, the second one running through these strawberry fields. I want to say the farm is Van Lierop's, but I know that isn't right. Picha's! That's the family's name. And hallelujah that their farm is still a farm. How rare is that these days? Too rare. Anyway, because it's a farm—muddy open land by the wide, wide acre—there's still a view: this ecstatic corridor with Mt. Rainier at the end of it, giant. You could parcel the view into subdivisions and sell it 900 times, become a zillionaire, only you can't, not without making it worthless. See, you need that *nothing-in-the-way-ness* for the view to be the view: a snow-capped volcano that just keeps rising.

Fourteen.

Thousand.

Feet.

Developers might see it differently, but they'd be wrong. My friend Jamie put it perfectly: "Mt. Rainier gets overlooked in a traffic jam. Even though you actually have more time to look at it." How much more so in a human jam of identical three-bedroom boxes? More than I want to think about, so I won't. I'd rather wonder what the mountain is thinking.

When it's looking down over the valley of us, out west toward Puget Sound, I bet it thinks our strawberry fields are an odd but glad addition. Our sprawl and neon graffiti not so much.

CHOCOLATE, COFFEE, SHEEP, & MAPS

I drive our son Jameson to school, and sometimes I have the radio tuned to Morning Edition on National Public Radio. The timing is pretty good because now and then, around 8:45, I'll catch a four-minute segment by a woman who's an expert on trees.

Anyway, back in March she was talking about where chocolate comes from—cacao trees—and explaining that their seed pods grow straight from the trunk. That's rare. Usually, seed pods hang from the branches, but in the cacao's case, they need the help of howler monkeys, and those things weigh about thirty pounds—too much for the cacao's slender limbs to keep from snapping—so the trees evolved. They needed the monkeys to break open their seed pods and eat and drop them (reproduction), and that meant the seed pods needed to grow from the trunk. How frickin' cool is that?

And why would anyone think that they can do a better job than nature?

THE SHEPHERD AND THE TECH CONSULTANT

One day a shepherd saw a man approaching. The man was sporting new boots, a Tyrolean hat.

The shepherd was wary, of course, used to sensing things from a distance, and able to tell when birds-turned-quiet meant *bear*, or *storm*, or *who knows but better keep an eye on this*. She was wary, even annoyed, but she waved hello.

"I thought you'd be a man," the man said, "and have a stick with a curly-cue hook," but she didn't shoot yet. Her gun was for emergencies.

Still, she wished that the wind would pick up, howl loud so she couldn't hear him talking: About optimizing grazing with his chewing algorithm, and improving sheep cognition with his evolution software, and enriching the softness of their wool with his image-filter comb, a comb now killing it in Phase Two beta-testing, a comb whose code lines were written by secret monks kept hidden with a cloaking program hacked from NASA engineers. "Just think of the sweaters," he said, "and what they could do for Humanity"—

Once the echoes died down and the birds had resettled, the woods gave thanks by seeming greener. She could smell November—smoke gone, a certain cleanness. And no one in town would mind that she'd had to shoot a wolf.

Of course, artificiality is not the only problem. Another is the false promise of a shortcut. Those suckers are enticing, aren't they? Even though they're synonyms for *mirage*?

That's sort of what this next one's about. That, and the goodness of coffee:

THE MAPMAKER'S STORY
Thing is, she understands people:
everyone looking for a shortcut.

So she draws them a road—
finally paved, but snake-narrow—

and a trestle bridge
to mark the turn.

The switchbacks
are going to be insanity,

and the drop-offs
steeper than they're thinking,

and she leaves out the part about logging trucks
always hauling ass around a curve.

You can't draw fog on a map,
so she doesn't,

but she highlights the fork ahead in red:
either over the pass to the interstate,

or this way brings them back
and she'll have the coffee waiting.

If people want to measure things in miles,
well, that's up to them.

SEVEN BIRDS

Northeast of Salt Lake City
Higher up the Wasatch Mountains, just outside of Heber, you can see these fledgling eagles learning to fly. They take turns swooping, landing in the meadow, then letting loose with an eagle *shriek* or *Amen*. And no, I can't do impressions, can't name each bone in their wings, but I can tell you for certain that the grasslands below them have mice, and also just a few more years before they're gone, become in-fill, the suburbs covering the valley, the suburbs like a new sort of glacier made of plastic and cul-de-sac tar.

The Outskirts of Sydney
I'll admit it was 37 years ago, so by now things might have changed, but the only McDonald's I remember is this one in the suburbs of Sydney, Australia. Their hamburgers didn't come with ketchup—you had to buy that extra—and they didn't call it ketchup:
    "Oh, you mean sauce?"
    "Yeah, sure. Tomato sauce. How much for that?"
    The rest was the usual—the uniforms, the furniture, even the straws—despite the Date Line, and the upside-down-ness of the hemisphere, and the alien patterns of the constellations, and we'd driven on the wrong side to get there, and I was the one with the accent, and the teenage guys called the teen girls "birds." But McDonald's was the same.

In Our Garden
I was out weeding the garden. My wife Jen was cleaning the garage.
    "Hey, you might want to see this," I said. "There are quail."
    The male was nearby, just a couple feet away, calling out and ignoring me. And the female was three plots behind me, ignoring him.

"She's got chicks," Jen said.

They were chittering under the sunflowers, probably eating the seeds since there are lots, more than the birds can finish, so some take root, grow back, become the first green action in April: *volunteers*—that's what it's called when they do that—plants that you don't have to plant. Look around: sunflowers everywhere, leaning over the fence between the day-care playground and the vacant lot, and jumping from front yards to medians, then on down the block. . . a take-over, sure, but with waving.

And never that same kind of yellow as parking lot stripes.

Purdy, Washington

I, too, would like a cabin there, with a footpath down to the oyster-shell beach, where some days, looking for hermit crabs, I might see herons come gliding. . .

Great Blue. With their eight-foot wingspans. Taking fish, or not, from this narrow end of the inlet.

What an arrangement of angles.

Who can beat that?

Next Door to My House

My neighbor told me there are people who still eat doves. I don't know if I believe him.

He's got a box in his tree for kestrels, though, so probably.

The 21st Century

There's that scene—remember?—at the end of *Jurassic Park*, where the ones not eaten are rescued, and Dr. Grant looks out of the helicopter window, smiling at a flight-line of pelicans, his hypothesis confirmed: *Dinosaurs aren't extinct; they just escaped into adaptation.*

And so could we. At least I think so, because I'm not a science-denying ostrich. Climate extremes, extreme weather—these are real. But so is our ability to change things.

The Kitchen Counter Where I'm Writing This

It's almost time for another Thanksgiving, when the President will pardon a turkey; it's tradition. Another is saying what you're thankful for, so here goes:

To the birds who make our neighborhoods their neighborhoods as well, who lend their songs and *ya-honks* to the morning. And to seagulls—what good is a shoreline without you? The sky would be missing its dancers, and the wind a one-note orchestra. To the blue jays yelling at everyone from fence posts; and roosters doing your farm-strut; and the childhood robins of my Washington, constant as the rain. To you hawks above our freeways who leave roadkill-picking to magpies—you don't wait for an afterlife, you soar right now, seeing much farther than we do. To peacocks forever looking Mardi Gras; and to owls, you Ministers of Silence; and to you, the birds in my future, let me say thanks.

And thanks yesterday.

And thanks again tomorrow.

May all of you be well.

ENVIRONMENTAL STUDIES

Washington

Washington's state bird is the goldfinch, but as a kid growing up there I always thought that seemed wrong. Robins you saw everywhere, especially after rain, hopping around and unspooling the worms from the lawn— night crawlers long as a shoelace—but goldfinches? Almost never. They were mostly just pictures in books.

Utah

So imagine my surprise last month when I spotted a goldfinch in my Salt Lake City yard. No, two. . . no, three. . . wait, there's another one. Four.

Parent with fledglings? Boyfriend and girlfriends? I wasn't sure. One had vivid feathers, black and yellow. The other three were more muted, with coloring less like exclamation points.

I'd been reading the Friday *Salt Lake Tribune*, skimming the recaps of politics, and was heading out to clear the wind-snapped branches from the yard, and there they were, riding these wire-thin tensile stems that rise up near the sidewalk, see-sawing on the ends and eating the flowers, or maybe just the bugs on the flowers, I don't know. What I do know is they didn't give a crap about the republican political agenda.

Political Climate

"First-ism"; trans., "isolationism." Always forever hollering about this: banning Muslims, rounding up aliens (their word, not mine), talk of shaking down NATO for protection money, reneging on international trade pacts, and tweets about reneging on more, and so on.

A lot gets said about the ethical/economic sinkhole this will cause, but I don't hear much about it being bad for the environment, and it is. The environment isn't American, isn't an our-side/your-side attitude. I mean, who's going to work with us on long-term fixes if we've traded away good will for an unfounded claim on a baseball hat?

Utah

The day I saw those goldfinches was another in a long stretch of 100+ degrees. And there were algal blooms too, turning water into warnings, with signs going up along the shorelines, basically saying: STAY AWAY OR THIS WILL KILL YOU.

Add air-pollution advisories and other examples year 'round, and we should be concerned.

U.S.A.

Each state knows what I'm talking about. We can't deport rising temperatures. We can't turn our backs on the water and the air.

My House

I'm dodging a moth while I write this, which strikes me as kind of funny. It's drinking the condensation, I think, off the can of Rainier beside me on the table, then berzerking its way from lamp to lamp, then coming back to flap in my face, in my ear, then finally land in the crook of my elbow. It's as graceless as those goldfinches were graceful, and I'm glad I got to see them. They aren't commonplace in Utah, but even the worst ornithologist would never call them "aliens." And this moth on my beer is a nuisance, yes, but I like it way more than I like anti-immigrant politicians.

Political Climate

Did you see that? Somehow it seeped in again, politics like Thought Smog, when all I wanted was to offer you a poem. It's environmental, and it goes like this:

THE MOTHER OF THE MOUNTAINS

If a mama bear gets angry, imagine the Mother of the Mountains.
Mess with Her children, She'll dust off an avalanche;

step out of line,
She'll realign your bones.

She's a blue-eyed beauty,
and the mountains have their Mother's eyes: deep lakes.

Gaze into them, you'll see their thoughts like fish—
quick schools, slow rainbows—look deeper,

and you'll learn to dream
like a stone.

What does She feed them? Rain for breakfast.
Anything else? She peels them the sun for lunch.

And at night? Big helpings of quiet,
then the Mother of the Mountains sings them to sleep with snow.

The trees are Her grandkids; She brings them birds to play with.
Whenever it's their birthday, She gives them an owl

'cause though She's a blue-eyed beauty, She's still kind,
even soft, even fragile.

Wolves howl to Her to show their gratitude.
What about you?

TWO JOBS

1.

Over the years, I've had my fair share of pretty odd jobs. I worked the graveyard shift in a pickle factory, delivered fireworks to parking-lot fireworks stands, answered the phone as a tutor for this high school kid up in Noatak, Alaska, and these private school prepsters at some place called Pillow Academy in Mississippi.

Bagging groceries? Yep.

Umpire for six-year-old T-ball games? Yep again, and who knew parents could be so invested? *Come on, Ump! Get your eyes checked, dimwit! My kid is being scouted by the New York Yankees!*

How about loading panel trucks at the warehouse hub in Spokane? I did that too, also on the graveyard shift, like I was some kind of low-wage vampire, loading trucks for United Parcel while the northside suburbs were under construction; meaning, every night new street names popped up on the map—Lake Street, Lake Court, Lake Route, Lake Place, Lake Lane, Lakeside Boulevard, Lakeview Circle, Lake Vista Avenue—and each one had its own designated space on the shelves.

Oh, and I also had a manager, a manager whose job seemed to be to just follow me around. I'd run back and forth from the conveyor belt to a panel truck with this dipshit shadow over my shoulder, with this ass-clown behind me like a backpack, and all the time shouting his mantra in my ear: "Work harder, work faster." I want to say I punched his fucking face in for him, but no.

And then there was this one—not a job, exactly, but it felt like one. I was home for Christmas, and my mom had this to say: "People I know think you're funny. I don't think you're funny at all. Say something funny."

31

"You mean, now?"

"Yeah, right now. Let's see if I laugh."

I wasn't successful.

So anyway, jobs—maybe you've had a few doozies too. But some jobs are way too important to quit, like migration and being the moon:

"It's Time, It's Time, It's Time"
Hello, migration—bird after bird,
pushing the wind around.

Down here the moss is still green,
but I follow your point, and I like your honking.

There's always more work to do, isn't there?
It's getting cold.

2.

When I lived in Spokane in the 1990s, I didn't mind the lights, so I didn't close the blinds. But one night I woke up, and the light in my room was bright red, like the building across the street might be on fire and I should get the hell out of there.

It wasn't on fire, though. In fact, nothing in the city was in flames—just a strange rectangular glow about a half a mile away. I put on my glasses, looked again, and saw this giant block-lettering, hideous, that spelled, "BUFFET." How pathetic is that? Extremely.

Not that I got dressed and went and shattered the sign with rocks, but I absolutely thought about it. And I still believe it would've been the right thing to do:

"Open 24 Hours"
Our moon wasn't born
to look down at neon skies.

That was never in its forecast.
It can glow. And it predicts the tides,

those blue-green birthdays
always arriving.

It can pass for one minnow in the universe,
and yet still tell the sun, "Hold on,

just keep sitting in the east,
you aren't the driving song of astronauts.

I'm a medium,
the strange lines in their palms,

but to look at you
is to blink."

No wonder the moon
used to fire our legends.

What made us think
we can confiscate the night?

TWO OBSERVATIONS

1.

I hope you'll excuse me for thinking that the whole space tourism trend was concocted by a-holes. But anything that exclusive—only affordable to zillionaires—what else can I say? Plus, the rest of us are the *real* space tourists, just by looking up, assuming we can leave the city for a night, that we can aim for somewhere open, get out and drive, pull over and park, then start counting the Perseid meteors by their burn-trails, brief and white. Sometimes they're by The Big Dipper, sometimes Orion, others not; sometimes they're nearer to whatever that cluster is—Who knows, until we give it a name?

"That M-shape, there, is The Raven."

"See the arc of five above a brighter dot? I'm pretty sure that one's The Hieroglyph Eye."

"And those four, lowest in the sky, are called The Boat since they sail the horizon."

My wife Jen keeps track of upcoming eclipses. She's a better space tourist than a million multi-millionaires. And me, I'm some kind of tourist, too, since I remember when you didn't have to drive somewhere to see them. Not a space tourist, no, but possibly a tourist of time. . .

> EVERY PLACE I'VE EVER LIVED IS GONE:
> all the orchards south of Salt Lake City,
> the pine woods north of Spokane,
>
> the field by my house where the snow piled deep,
> where a snow owl passed so silently and low

it changed my idea of ghosts—
now they're stores,

and neighborhoods named after trees,
and spillover parking for a church,

and maybe the choir sings hymns so beautifully
it's fine; I'll call it the future, agree that it's bright.

But west of Washtucna, Washington,
the highway stretches through the dark. . .

miles of *no-place*, of *in-between*,
that haven't disappeared.

Freight trucks are too few to bother me much,
and wind off the river cools the hood down.

I can stop on the shoulder and sit there still
while stars fill every inch of night.

2.

The wind thinks smithereening tool sheds is funny. My dad had a tool
shed when I was a kid, and the morning after a windstorm, it was gone.
Or it was *almost* gone. The wind had wadded it up like paper, then tossed
it over our house and into the ditch, like the wind was just playing a game
of garbage-can basketball.

Here's another example: Before Jen and I were married, she had a rental
house up in the foothills east of the city, a house with a shed, the same
kind my dad had, and one day a windstorm swept down the mountain
and changed it into a jagged mangle.

If you think that afterward her landlord said, "I'll handle it," think
again.

"Pull it apart and haul it to the curb," he told her. "You can use my tools," he said, which were a hammer and a mismatched pair of gloves.

Or try setting up a seasonal fireworks stand in a parking lot in Lewiston, Idaho: The panels are sheet metal, black, and it's 99 degrees; and they're 8' x 8', so at least a hundred pounds; and the wind starts blowing like some dragon-breath laughter; and those panels, when you try to stand them up, just catch it like sails; you can't let go, but you'd better. A dilemma, but worse, and also faster.

I'm saying the wind is our friend until it isn't. We need it, but it doesn't need us:

"FOR YOUR ESSAY, DESCRIBE NATURE"
The screen door batters in its frame.
This is no June storm,

it's more
than a little wind,

so stand with your back against
whatever swear words you can.

Let them bloom.
Plant a garden.

If you had peaches, they'd be
flinging, nothing left:

wind-pilfered, engined
under.

You can lovetalk forever about nature.
It'll still kick your ass.

A QUESTION FOR THE ANTI-SCIENTISTS

When I was growing up, the weather reports always seemed to track and update the snowfall in Buffalo, New York. How many feet so far? How many inches on top of that today? Like Buffalo's snow was the baseline for the nation.

Not anymore. Our oldest son, Ozzly—he lives in New York City—was home for Christmas. It wasn't a white Christmas in Salt Lake this year, and it wasn't in New York either, and when Oz checked the temperature in Buffalo, it was 54 degrees.

In fact, the whole country is warmer than the forecasters can remember, which might not sound too bad to someone, but here in Utah, you could say I'm a little freaked out. Last year's snow was like a miracle (I mean, our governor had actually issued a statewide "plan" for people to pray about having the drought end), but we're back to zero snow again, and the Great Salt Lake is on the clock: five years to extinction.

Anyway, I do have a question, and I'll get to it in a minute—right after this poem and a few observations:

HE STARTS HIS MORNING WITH COFFEE,
then flips the news on
to hear what the satellites are saying.

They're up there in orbit
where the rockets shot them years ago:

Some kind of protest again,
parents pissed off at a School Board,

yelling and stomping with their picket signs—
"Can't spell science without S-I-N"—

and, of course, that's pretty irrefutable.
So he prays that God will punish the doctors,

stoke up the coals under Darwin.
"And maybe," he adds,

"if there's some time left over,
send another earthquake to Caltech."

Then he hops in the shower,
but the water's cold, and he's sad.

I like dramatic irony. It's fun, it's funny, and the audience knows which character doesn't get it. But while that's helpful in poems and plays, it isn't in life.

In life, you wish the person would get a clue, wise up, feel internally smacked by an epiphany.

In life, you wish they would trip and splat in what Aristotle called *anagnorisis*, which isn't mud; it's a sudden recognition that they were wrong and want to start over again, beginning this time with the knowledge that they possess now. How great would that be?

Instead, we're stuck with people who just persist.

Observation 1

Take the place where I live—Utah—and this year's legislative session. Back in February, we heard something hopeful for a minute. State Representative Andrew Stoddard (Democrat) introduced an air quality bill to cut bromine and chlorine emissions. It's a good idea. The winter inversions here trap smog so dense that you can't see the mountains from the valley, smog we breathe.

The only ones who might object, you'd think, would be the U.S. Magnesium Corporation, but they didn't. Nope, no squad of Headlock Lobbyists was speedily dispatched. In fact, "U.S. Magnesium's Director of Technical Services told Fox 13, 'I don't think the bill is going to change anything [for us]. It's a minor detail for U.S. Magnesium to report bromine.'" Even so, Representative Tim Jimenez (Republican) amended the bill, turning it into something that would "order further study," which, of course, is just codespeak for punting.

Observation 2

There was this one also: Utah House Bill 469, updated by Senator Scott Sandall (Republican). It nixes the state's current (not good) regulations on hunting mountain lions and replaces them with an even crappier plan to harvest (not my word for it) however many mountain lions they want to all year 'round, with no limits on the death count and no tag required.

People who know things—university researchers, wildlife biologists—would have said this is a horrible idea, which is probably why they weren't consulted and why the lawmakers went ahead and did it "with zero public input by slipping an amendment into an unrelated bill at the last hour."

Observation 3

Worst, though, is the non-plan to save the Great Salt Lake. House Majority Leader Mike Schultz (Republican) had this to say about it on Fox 13: "We need to look at everything under the sun. We're the fastest growing state in the nation. We can't just stop growing, right? [. . .] Are there things we can do, and can we do a better job shepherding water to the lake? Absolutely. That's what we need is a balanced approach."

If what you're thinking now is *What?* then you're not alone. For starters, that word-mush isn't a plan. And then there's this: One thing "under the sun to look at" has to be an end to sprawl, but Leader Schultz just assumes that constant growth is a given. I *do* like the part where we get to be Water Shepherds, but there are water shepherds already; they're called "rivers."

The problem is their water gets diverted and doesn't reach the lake. Plus, we all know that "balanced approach" means "more of the same."

Observation 4

The common denominator here is dissing science. Into microphones (which come from science). In front of TV cameras (more science). Kitchen refrigerators, microwave popcorn, the vulcanized rubber on the cars we drive, saving a life in a hospital, email requests to make a campaign donation, the lightbulbs and switches in the House and Senate—*all* of these things are more science.

So, what's the deal?

FEELING ISN'T A CHOICE, IT'S EVERYONE'S JOB

I'm not a hydrologist, but I still know how to use a water glass. If you drink it down halfway, and then more, and then almost to the bottom, then the only way to have more is to fill it back up.

Same with the Great Salt Lake: Divert the rivers that flow to it so that people in all the new housing tracts can have faucets and ice cubes and lawns, and there you go—little, less, and then nothing left to reach the lake. Which is why it's dying. Which is why we'll soon have nothing but a crust of salt and toxic dust, dust stirred up into every breath of air.

Our legislature knows this. They have reports. But in January 2023, they got a better report. . . well, more of a letter, but still. . . a letter that says this catastrophe is all the fault of trees.

Yep. That's exactly what I thought too.

Trees, it says—and this explains why several legislators signed on; a lot of them are developers—anyway, trees are out there drinking up the water, and *that's* why the lake is so low. So the obvious fix is to bulldoze and burn them, and as soon as we do—*Abracadabra!*—the lake will be restored.

I could go on trying to persuade you why this is dumb, but you already know that. And the problem, I think, with another essay is that anyone who doesn't know, or doesn't want to, isn't reading or listening anyway. So instead, sometimes I write parables—those old stories with setting and characters in action, those old stories that hope to demonstrate—because maybe stories still have a chance to find a different door, a doorway into people's thoughts, a doorway to reach their feelings for a minute, and that's how long most parables tend to be—no longer than a minute or two—but with an impact, perhaps, that lasts longer, that goes on growing inside someone the way a tree keeps growing rings.

Stories—especially fables, parables, and origin stories—have always played a role in our human understanding. Stories helped people define who they were and what they valued, helped create collective meaning, expressed reverence or issued warnings, connected the present to the past and tomorrow, and I believe they still can.

In fact, on the news just now as I've been typing this, a woman was asked, "How'd you do that?" (meaning, get donations of school supplies for every kid in her district), and she said, "Well, with the faith of a mustard seed, I started out, and the community just gathered around," which proves my belief in two ways. First, she reached for a parable. But second, not everyone measures life by Matthew, Mark, Luke, and John; not everyone knows her allusion or compares the present to such long-ago stories. Instead, what we need are new ones.

So here are three:

The first one, "The Story of the Cook," isn't about the Great Salt Lake. It's about the people who give and the ones who keep on taking, and because my wife is a fifth-grade teacher (and my parents were teachers, and a lot of my friends' parents were teachers), I think of this cook as a teacher in disguise, in quiet metaphor.

You're free, of course, to think of someone else who gives. Parables intend for you to do that. They're aiming at universality rather than the singular and literal. Take that naked emperor, for instance. He isn't just one idiot who's naked and an emperor. And the kid pointing out that the emperor is a dumbass isn't just one kid. They could be anyone and everyone by design. Same with this cook, and with the people who always keep coming, wanting more:

THE STORY OF THE COOK

A day or two after the cook moved in, everything started to change. Each morning, the people lined up on her porch to ask please: for the pies that their grandmothers made, and huge birds stuffed with plums and acorns, the lasagna he'd had once somewhere in Montana—an improbable place, he agreed, but "*Good God*, the sauce, and those cheeses, and trees that went all the way up to a summer-colored sky."

"If you could make us *that*," they all said.

And so she did.

It was good to be generous, spending nights at her table writing recipes, using weekends to hunt for mushrooms tucked between moss, and mud, and a stump she might have sat on if only there were time.

That was her secret, her ingredient: adding time from her own past and future. Adding time while the mirror grew thinner around her every day, until she faded, and finally was gone, just a faint trace of cinnamon.

That's why the people need a new cook now. That's why they're painting and hanging up a "Help Wanted" sign.

Now, this second parable isn't directly about the Great Salt Lake either; that'll be the third one. But it does approach the lake's crisis, or at least one major cause of it:

THE STORY OF THE FARMER

It's hard work, meeting the needs of a region, so each day the farmer rose at four. He ate toast, poured another cup of coffee, then checked on his clouds, the cirrus and stratus, the acres of temperamental cumulus—all there stirring in their sleep, but all of them fine, maybe dreaming that the rooster wouldn't crow.

If a cloud was ready to harvest, the farmer fastened a string, and his sheepdog, Mary, watched it lift with maternal concern, watched it rise, catch the wind, and take the slack the farmer kept spooling out. Then he'd fasten a string to another so there would be rain, enough that even ferns could grow, and buds could appear between bricks in the cobblestone walks from back doors to gardens. Enough for streambeds to know they had a purpose, for the sun to seem brighter by contrast, and for robins on lawns throughout town to do their thing, pulling worms from the ground—*Hop-stab, Hop-stab.*

A good life, and meaningful, if it weren't for the insurance: the lightning that had to be indemnified, and the supplemental policies in case of broken hearts if his rain was too beautiful, too lonely.

There were the ones, as well, needing land to build more *everything*.

"What would be the price," they all kept asking, "to leash your dog, cut ties, and walk away?"

And this is the third parable. I think three makes sense since it's a biblically important number and the word "parable" reminds many people of Sunday School. That's fine—and it's one of the reasons I hope parables can reach a wider audience—but, to me, *ethics* are what matter because they're human derived through human reasoning:

THE WOMAN WHO KEPT ON TALKING

The woman kept talking in the plaza, even at night when all but the cats had gone home. The people had suppers to eat. There were things on TV.

She had wind in her hair and wrapped around her, but still the woman talked.

After days in the sun, she must have been thirsty, but her voice kept on like the memory of water, always there.

Sometimes a few would make a game of it, waving hands in front of her eyes to see if she would blink. They said that her eyes were quite beautiful.

Not that the ones playing chess would ever notice. Not the bakers at their shop counters either, their aprons dusted with flour and all the hours of intricate sugar; she was too far to see, and they didn't care anyway.

Crows, however, kept her company, so some said her talking was witchcraft. Others complained that the woman ought to be at home, or at work, or just somewhere else and quiet, but she didn't stop. She kept on talking. . . past the hour when her megaphone batteries died, past the month the last forest in the West caught fire, past the year the Great Salt Lake disappeared, became dust, and the dust choked the wind, and the wind had a voice, some said, that seemed almost familiar, like the voice of that woman who had kept on talking.

Even in the box they'd built and shut her inside.

Circling back, then, to the title—"Feeling Isn't a Choice, It's Everyone's Job"—I think new parables can make that job a little easier. First, because the oral tradition is still with us (think "podcasts"). And second, because this old form is archetypal. The *form* is familiar, but people haven't heard these plots before, so hopefully they'll want to stay and read in order to see what happens. Then maybe leave changed.

Which brings me to the benediction:

THE HOUSEPAINTER'S STORY
Since he works with invisible paint,
he knows complaints are part of the bargain.

They go outside to check the mail,
and the house seems gone behind them;

or they park out front along the curb,
and nothing's there—just a view

from the car to the garden. . .
The housepainter knows not everyone's a fan.

Most come around, though, once they notice
their walls are all sightlines,

once they see their roofs are like sky again,
nothing in the way. And now, look:

The mountains are returning,
stepping closer to the edge of the city.

And the buildings—those rectangle blinders—
have disappeared.

IN THE BEGINNING WAS A RIVER

People who know me know this: I don't pretend to be an expert on the legal codes of New Zealand.

But back in March something happened there that keeps on running through my mind. Their House of Representatives, which must be a whole bunch different than ours, passed a bill giving human rights to the Whanganui River. How's that for treatment of a natural resource? Pretty good.

And what I keep thinking—now that a river can claim personhood and dignity—is, what do I want to suggest for human rights next?

Probably stars. They deserve to be noticed. Once a month we'll have darkness by decree. We'll have twelve new nights to look up, a dozen needed oases.

And Puget Sound, of course. Whether seen from a ferry or not. Whether or not it's sundown on Seattle's million windows so the skyline is mirroring gold-orange, rose, and red. And the Olympic Mountains are both in front of you and behind you. And seagulls ride rivers of updraft. And this time and place and wind should be vested with rights.

The trees near Crescent City too—they're older than Christianity. I'll call each redwood a cathedral, drinking fog, which truly is Holy Water.

The snowmelt I drank in an ice cave: rights.

Those ghost-conversations of coyotes: rights.

That soul-blown sound of a train at night—part love, part loss, and part Coltrane—couldn't be more human, with the human right to quiet, so that everyone who needs to hear can hear.

And what about you? Isn't there a lakeshore somewhere? Or a night in some December? Or a time you saw some pronghorn and were doubly surprised—first by their nearness, then a second time by how they leapt away: too squat to be bounding like that? Isn't there a long-distance drive you've taken with a good enough reason at the end of it? Or a view from the porch of a lightning storm coursing the sky?

Anyway, it's April, soon to be summer in Utah, where most aren't yelling and opposed to helping refugees. Most don't think it's okay to zero them out, leave them trapped in their national horrors.

In New Zealand they've granted more rights than that to a river, which ought to be an elemental lesson.

Here's hoping it flows all the way from there to D.C.

II.

WINE IS RAIN IN TRANSLATION

POETRY

The poem is a shapeshifter animal, a trickster.
One minute, it's a sailfish. The next, it's a hook.

One night, it's an alley cat, urgent to get you outdoors,
get you on the fire escape and screaming. Another, it sleeps.

I remember there was a great migration—
poems soaring home.

And I remember, too, when they used to thunder like trains,
crushing the grass.

I watched as the herd turned into crickets. . . then rain. . .
then into kids in the backyard, running for the house

before the raindrops turned into hail, and while I watched
I smelled my dinner burning. Clever trick.

"Well, what's the good in that?" Not much.
"Then what the hell's it want?" I don't know—to astonish

like leaves do in autumn. To hope, I guess,
it says one small thing that lasts.

I'd prefer to leave it at that, to add nothing, since going on now means
reducing the poem to an epigram, as if prose were really the bigger-stakes

work, and I don't want to concede that. But back in mid-September, my friend Joe Roberts wrote me a note that I've been thinking about ever since.

He said, "I have a question for you. I've been struggling to come up with a purpose for poetry as opposed to prose. What makes poetry's purpose distinctive?"

Thank you, Joe. It's nice being thought of as a guy who might have an answer.

On the one hand, I'm not sure poems have to have a purpose. I mean, I'd rather have lamps be lamps and let poems be the occasional genie. On the other hand, I know that's ridiculous. Poems *do* have purposes, lots of them, and I shouldn't avoid adding my thoughts about what those purposes are just because doing so takes some work. I know this won't be my final answer—there will be days ahead when I think of others, then others after that—but here goes: Joe said he'd been reading *Spring and All* (William Carlos Williams). He said Williams' ideas were pretty good. He said, "The definition I pulled from him is that prose is meant to serve the emotions and be representational. Poetry is meant to serve the imagination and create something truly new. It's not a mirror to hold up to nature; it is an addition to nature, a 'crystallization of the imagination.'"

Now, I love Williams by the acre, by the square mile, but I'm going to have to say I think he's probably wrong about that one. Take Faulkner's *Go Down, Moses*. It's prose not poetry, and it's truly new. And that's just one example. In fact, it's the first one that popped into my head.

Here's another: Pick any of a dozen albums by Bob Dylan; what's happening seems both true and new to me, and also different than a poem, or even a whole book of poems, since there's the added interplay of voice and instruments to go along with whatever story, or character, or philosophical headlock he's turned into lyrics.

No, probably the rightest part of Williams' idea is the "crystallization" thing. Faulkner gives us whole caves full of stalactites, stalagmites, bats, pooling water old as Original Sin, and also crystals; yet, love that as much as you want, you can't wear it around your neck. Same with Dylan. Sure, he's bardic, but how long do you think it took the roadies to unload and set up for every concert on, say, his Rolling Thunder Revue tour in 1975? What's different (distinct) about poems, I think, isn't fancy. It's that they're short.

I said this once to Tony Weller, a bookseller in Salt Lake City. At first he thought I was a spluttering dunce, or just being lazy about the question. But I halfway talked him around to my point of view: Poems are short, even when halfway behaving like narratives, even when they're sharing a compact story. They're crystallized: the heart's psalm, the mind's wind chimes.

I'm saying—and yes, I started this by saying the opposite ("Do I contradict myself? / Very well then I contradict myself, / I am large, I contain multitudes"; Walt Whitman)—I'm saying that the distinction of poetry is *its ability to be epigrammatic.* You can carry a poem inside you like a talisman because you can remember it completely, start to finish, word for word. And it doesn't need accompaniment, just you, reciting the lines and the rhythms, all its images and meanings, meanings you might start to paraphrase, and then decide that you don't really need to after all.

LYNX MUSIC
The lynx knows all about quiet,
his ears grown long to hear more of it.

He sharpens his claws on the trunk of it,
hunts silence,

carries it home. And his paws
ghost over snowdrifts,

and lakes are asleep
under ice sheets,

and the stars seem frozen
like an orchestra, waiting to begin. . .

Has anyone seen the conductor?
Where has she gone in her night tuxedo?

The lynx looks ready to tell us something,
but only in the speech of violins.

EVOLUTION

My friend Jason asked me what I thought of a poem he'd just written. He was on a train somewhere, headed back to Brooklyn—this was through email—and I told him I liked it but might change a couple phrases.

He said, "Thanks but I'm thinking I need to blow the whole thing up and make it much weirder," that it was too much like "the imitation of a poem rather than an actual poem."

That's the sort of savvy stuff I'm used to from him, and it made me start running through my own Inventory of the Weird, like I'm lab-testing his hypothesis.

It checks out. For instance, the movie *Tin Cup* was on TV yesterday, and my favorite part is still when Roy and his friend (and caddy) Romeo are getting out of Roy's old convertible Cadillac, and Romeo tells him, "I only got one rule, boss, and that's never bet money that you don't have on a dog race with an ex-girlfriend who happens to be a stripper, and you broke that rule, Holmes. Now you're gonna have to be sweet to her." This dialogue isn't plot-centric at all. It's just there. Weirdness that levitates.

Another example: I spent two nights in Hamilton, Montana, as a guest being taken care of by strangers. One night I stepped out onto the back stoop and almost into a porcupine. It was there, maybe a foot away, eating out of the dog dish. I stood still, and thought about stillness, until it finally settled its quills back down and plodded off between the apple trees. Now, who cares what happened on the other night?

Or take New York City, where Jason lives, and not porcupines but Frank O'Hara. O'Hara's got a poem ("Personal Poem") about hanging out with his friend Leroi Jones, and he mentions the construction on all the corners and girders of Manhattan, saying, "If / I ever get to be a construction worker / I'd like to have a silver hat please." Who's he talking to—himself? the reader? some imaginary god of hard hat dispersal? It doesn't matter. It's a goofball outburst of weirdness.

I think what I mean—what Jason meant too—is that weirdness can also be an evolution.

If you don't believe me, go and look at a moose. Did you know they can close their nostrils and stay underwater like these algae-grazing submarines? You don't get weirder than an anglerfish, but it works. What's got more style, a cow or a longhorn?

It's the same thing with writing. Weird is good.

WINE IS RAIN IN TRANSLATION

Wine is rain in translation. And corkscrews are lines in translation. And glasses are sand in translation, sometimes on stems. How great would it be if we could plant them, watch them turn and lean toward the sun?

I've been thinking about translation for a while now, ever since *Terrain. org* published four Icelandic poems by Magnús Sigurdsson. There was something about the way they fit on the screen so that you couldn't see the English without scrolling down, and I decided I didn't want to. Not until I'd tried my own "translations" first.

My friend Rick suggested this years ago—trying to work out approximate versions in English based solely on the way another language looks: the pattern of letters, how you might pronounce them, and so on. Having no clue about the original was his only rule, and I definitely didn't. To me, the title of the first poem looked like "Origami Journey," assuming you could flip the adjective the way you would in Spanish. I dug that idea (*What's an origami journey?*), but the opening line, which looked a lot like "Kari's grandmother," hooked me more, so that's where I started.

Then the second line had something close to "put some scribbles there." And then a long word (a kenning?) in the fourth line looked like "it's-spring-again" all squished together. So I was in and kept on going.

It didn't matter that none of this was going to be right, not literally. Literally, the poem's about beetles. That wasn't the sort of translation I was up to, though, and I can't imagine that Magnús Sigurdsson would mind. He might even see it the same way I do: Sometimes it's not bad to bend things. The first slam dunk bent the sky and the future. Billie Holiday bent songs. And bending a straight line around and around amounts to

something that can uncork wine. All of us ought to try bending more.
So I did:

"ART IS SUCH A GOOD JOURNEY"
Kari's grandmother used to tell us,
"Put some scribbles there—

a million begonias.
And now it's spring again, blooming. Yes."

Not scuba,
not yoga,

not for her,
but she could make you young-eyed

when teaching you to paint.
"Orange pinwheels, try it,

that's sunlight,
that's Mama Eggs." And my favorite,

what I'll never forget:
"Don't ever put your vision on

like shoes, my darlings. We're traveling
not making doormats."

POETRY AS COLLAGE

"What Are Your Skills?"
Every year at Sea School
we were taught that glaciers purr

and ice floes, huge
below the surface, were sunning cats.

Call ours a failed education.
If it makes you feel better,

call our hymns under night skies
cracked.

But for thirteen years
we sailed on bluer water.

And all of us know well
how to arch our backs.

My favorite American artist is Romare Bearden. I especially love his collages. One called *Mill Hand's Lunch Bucket*, for example, led August Wilson (love him too) to write his play *Joe Turner's Come and Gone*. If I remember correctly, Wilson said that the haunted-looking figure seated in the center became his character Harold Loomis. For me, though, it's another figure coming down the stairs who makes the biggest impact. Out the window, we can see the dragon-fire and industry-teeth of smokestacks, and it's clear that this man is on his way to work there, and he's a normal-sized man, and the lunchbox on the boarding house table is normal-sized, but the man's hand is huge: his hunger, need, and soul so much bigger than the opportunities life as a Black man in a mill town will provide. It's Social-Realism; only to get there, Bearden ditches the realism.

I try to do that too, preferring myth, for instance, to confessional modes and sticking to the facts. And in the case of these two poems, I'm almost working in collage.

For example, "What Are Your Skills?" is my guess about what the Icelandic poet Magnús Sigurdsson's title "Vatnaskil" might be in English. And Icelandic words like "skolad," "mér," "purrt," "hugarfljótid," and "Undir nyjum / himni" became the fragments I combined into a Sea School, ice floes, purring cats, and hymns sung under night skies. Even better, my poem became a talking back to the ruling half of our country, and I swear that's because I set out to write while brain-blind; instead of having an editorial subject, I had mystery and questions.

That's even truer of the next poem. At first I only had the title ("Vetrarhugar") and the opening lines, "Pad hefur gránad / í fjöll," which looked to me like, "Paul's grandfather fell." The bonus was that I don't know anyone named Paul, so I could just be an oracle:

"ARE YOU HUNGRY?"
Paul's grandfather fell from his house in the air
when his dreaming turned to birds.

Sometimes it means you'll find a hawk's egg,
and others it just means listen to the river

saying, "Start in my stream below the mountain's scar,
and ignore the bears around you.

Float still, a leaf, then find
momentum. You'll gain the whole sea."

Midnight visions are a common kind of travel,
whether *just a journey* or *a finding*.

But you can't peg orders, can't call the shots,
or dreams stall, lose power, maybe drop you

from your tree house. You'll land
in an empty kitchen, wanting bread.

These poems, of course, aren't actual collages; I know that. In an email, Magnús suggested an alternative term: "magnified or distorted collage, so to speak." That phrasing is fine with me, at least for now and unofficially, since a magnified tree would be a redwood, and distorted and magnified details are what I like about *Mill Hand's Lunch Bucket*.

Anyway, I hope these poems work similarly: zeroing in by distorting. And maybe they magnified a moment of your day.

WIN $300.00

I'll give a hundred bucks to the first person who correctly names the inventor of iambic pentameter. You can set aside reading this and call me with your answer (801-533-9887), but you have to do it now.

Three.

Two.

One.

No, it wasn't Shakespeare.

And no, not Chaucer either, although I've heard it said that he brought it back from Italy along with a copy of *The Decameron* and some horrible verse forms like the sestina.

I learned the answer years ago from an Irish poet named Jim McAuley. I was in Spokane, Washington, taking classes in what used to be a bank. One classroom was actually the former vault, with the huge door left there on its hinges. Crazy. And McAuley told us that iambic pentameter was just another thing that the English stole from the Irish, which had my attention even before he got to the origin story, which was this: It came from the blacksmiths' shops. It was the practice of the master smith to use a smaller hammer—*tap*—to show his apprentice where the heavier blow should go—*bang*. It took five of these tap-bangs to shape a sword (tap BANG, tap BANG, tap BANG, tap BANG, tap BANG), which was a plausible explanation. More importantly, though, it was a perfect story because it also explains couplet rhymes: two sides to a sword (one side; flip; then the other), then back again with the metal to heat in the forge.

As for the specific Irish poet. . . by then I'd forgotten to care. I didn't ask. And given the Irish tendency toward music, conversation, and story-telling as Art rather than scribbling-down-on-paper, determining which poet first took that ten-stress rhyming system from the blacksmith shop to the page is impossible. So I'll just say the inventor is Jim McAuley. And anyway, the *story* of it matters more than the *who*. Think about it, we can trace a lot of things precisely to their source, and then yawn. For instance, whoever invented Velcro probably has a load of boring specifics on Wikipedia, but I don't care enough to spend five seconds now and see. I'm much more interested in this question of invention, of *originality*. What does it mean?

Take me: I'm a writer, I'm originally from the Northwest, and I'm imprinted by place. So it's possible I've written things that were already "said" a thousand years ago in the carving of a totem pole, and it's possible those things were said a hundred years before that—by the wind, back when the future totem pole was still a sapling.

And where did the wind first hear those phrases? And where did that wind originate?

For another $200.00, you can phone me your guesses, but the answer is Washington or Ireland. Two fine places for stories, and the twins of green.

DOWNHILL SWITCHBACKS AHEAD

To anyone outside of Washington, my hometown is un-pronounceable: Puyallup. Heck, I even hear outsiders mispronounce Spokane (sounds like *can*, not *cane*), so good luck with my town, stranger.

But I actually lived outside the city limits, in Pierce County, so to make it easier I'll just say I grew up on South Hill and then tell you about two ways we used to get down. One was Woodland Avenue, a straight shot down to Pioneer Way in this mile-long, forty-degree angle. The other was 128th, I think, but that far out—to the cliff edge over the Orting Valley—who really knows? The roads out there were more of a memory map than a system of signs with street names. And unlike Woodland, the road to the Orting Highway was more like a snake's dream of dancing. It wound through the trees, so no sightlines. And no streetlights. And one time, no headlights either since the car I drove was an antique T-Bird with corroded dust for wiring; the lights just cut out at random. Wicked scary. My point is I loved those downhill turns, even while suddenly blind, so writing sonnets was probably inevitable.

Sonnets? Yes, sonnets. Yes, those poems with all the quiz-able rules. Don't worry, though, I'm not going to drill you, and the rule I like best is the simple one anyway: *Somewhere between the middle and the end, you have to turn.*

I just brought up iambic pentameter ("Win $300.00"), so hopefully talking about sonnets now makes sense. I've actually written gobs of them, although I hadn't imagined writing any beyond the one we were all assigned in high school, and I think it's got something to do with that road I used to love to drive: every line like a cliff edge, and no clear vision of what's coming, then a turn in the middle, then a switchback, then you're there—just across the railroad tracks at the stop-sign-final punctuation, where you look out across the valley at Mt. Rainier. Not bad for fourteen lines, and sometimes worth the trouble. Here's what I mean:

SOME THINGS HAVE ONE MEANING, SOME THINGS DON'T:
"I do," for instance, is conditional;
the truth, it turns out, is political;
and *equal* means that most have equally less.

But words are like elastic, and unless
you're careful not to stretch too far, they won't
snap back.

I know what it is to be in love,
and no one has the right to disapprove
of who I love. They might, but they'd be wrong.

What else? Our lives are loaned to us. Not long.
And not to pile up money. Not for power.
And how we pay that loan back *does* matter:

with interest, yes—with being interested,
by promising and keeping promises,
by caring more and minding much less instead.

Does it turn? You betcha. There's the word "But," for instance, right there in line four, which is a pretty important word in English since it signals a contrast or foreshadows tension. In this case, though, it isn't really the turn (it's more of a shimmy). The turn comes two lines later, after the words "snap back," and I apologize to anyone for whom that's already obvious (I call out during football games too, even though the refs can't hear me). And there's the rhyming, of course, and the use of meter, and sometimes enjambment past the ends of the lines so that things don't stack up like fourteen boring dishes, and if that's all just a bunch of jabber to you, I understand. The gist is this: Sonnets are like puzzles, and puzzles are cool.

Also, they're similar to argumentative essays but succinct as a fist. What do I mean? I mean their structure is familiar already, drilled into us by Composition classes and all the essays we had to write in school: Thesis ~ Antithesis ~ Synthesis; or, Sweep right ~ Counter-trap left ~ Play-action pass to the tight end over the middle. Or if chess is more your metaphor, then sonnets are like 64 squares within a square, but just as full of possibility. Plus, the meter and rhyme can amp up the impact, and even be memorable, which makes sonnets pretty effective as a way to make a point. But the thing I like best, as I've mentioned already, is the formal requirement to turn, to swerve, to switchback, yet still wind up in the right place (or a better place) by the end.

Here's another sonnet to round this out that hopefully comes close to that:

WHY WE HAVE CATS

Sometimes it's almost sad to know you're dying.
The old bed frame out in the front yard, tossed,

while the weekend joggers jog on by. . .
even all the squirrels uncurious.

The weeds don't care you're getting rid of things;
they're a million indifferent persistences.

Still, these are the jobs—the sorting and stacking,
the doing-what-you-can about the fence,

and so you do. But also love someone
as much as cats love sunlight: all afternoon

and then again the next day. Geniuses.
What's left on the to-do list? What's a list?

But what if it starts raining? We'll go in.
How do I know you love me? Here's my chin.

I'D RATHER BE A HAWK

Like me, my friend Jason hates sestinas. Here's what he wrote in a poem of his recently:

> I was at a party where
> someone read a sestina,
> and everyone jumped head-
> first into the bushes
> one floor down, the black
> stocking legs of the women
> waving in the crisp November air.

That cracked me up. I'll take some well-timed humor over 39 lines of repetition any day.

And it's not because I lack discipline or have a gap in my aesthetic. I could use the form if I wanted to. In fact, I have—just once, and ages ago—in a poem called "Pharaoh's Horse Trainer." He's haunted in his sleep by the same recurring nightmare: all those chariot horses drowning when the parted waters closed behind Moses. And each day he combs the Red Sea shoreline for their bones. For him, I figured, the sestina made sense: obsession/compulsion. But that's it. Most subjects aren't so traumatically stuck, so why bolt them to a form that is? I'd rather be a hawk or a tide pool or something; those are forms too.

Still, if you can't shake the feeling that sestinas are expected and that writing one is a measure of your skills, then you might like this. It's a form I invented and kept secret up until now, and here are the rules: First, you don't get 39 lines, just 14. Second, yes, you still use iambic pentameter.

Third, but no, you don't use end rhyme. Fourth, instead, your end words are recycled in set positions, like so—

> The morning wakes up tired and more <u>gray</u>, [1]
> just lifting the sun out of habit, like winding a <u>watch</u>. [2]
> Why bother? Nothing can get warm in this <u>wind</u>, [3]
> and the haze will go on blocking whatever <u>light</u> [4]
>
> tries reaching here—the stars, the moon, <u>daylight</u>, [4]
> all of it gone. Only the snow's not <u>gray</u>, [1]
> and it will be soon. . . grit sifting out of <u>wind</u>, [3]
> snow plows dragging their loads of sand. I've <u>watched</u> [2]
>
> it happen every day this week. I've <u>watched</u> [2]
> and listened to them grind along, orange <u>lights</u> [4]
> spinning a kind of spiral web as they <u>wind</u> [3]
> from block to block. And of course the roads are <u>gray</u>, [1]

—and the fifth rule is: In the last two lines, you return to the original order (1, 2, 3, 4) with 1 and 3 placed in the middle of the lines, and 2 and 4 at the ends. How cool is that? As cool as a hawk or a tide pool, especially since now you can switch things up and use synonyms in place of repetition:

> favorite <u>non-color</u> [1] of progress and <u>watchbands</u>. [2]
> Meanwhile, the <u>wind</u> [3] keeps yelling that we're not the <u>sun</u>. [4]

That's it. I call it the sestonnet. It has the virtue of being shorter. Fewer guests (and that's what your listeners are) will be working the latches on the exit windows.

Haiku, of course, are shorter still, and they can be nice sometimes, like someone seeing you and smiling. A haiku can be nice like *Hello* can be nice, or *Good-bye*:

You've heard sharks don't sleep?
Your heart should be seven sharks.
Hunting what? More heart.

WHAT WOULD YOU DO WITH A MINI CANOE?

One day my son up and told me, "Hey, Dad, I know a good job for you."

"Yeah?" I said. "What's that?"

He said, "A writer. You know, like a *real* one."

I didn't mind. Quentin was ten years old, and I knew what he meant. He meant a novelist, someone he'd heard of, like Rick Riordan, with minotaurs and lightning thieves and some real money earned from his work.

Poets—at least most of us—don't get paid, and not because we're purists about it. We wouldn't say no to dollars, pesos, euros, even drachmas if those are still spendable. Try it; offer a poet some money sometime, and then clock how many seconds it takes to hear "Yes" and "Wow" and "Thanks" and "You're amazing." Probably one.

I started thinking about this back in January, during the Australian Open—I miss Federer—because they kept running this Visit Melbourne TV commercial: a montage of iconic scenery along with a recitation of some ballad stanzas by the Australian poet E.J. Brady. It made me think: 1) From now on every commercial has to be like this. Make TV stop it with its idiotic screaming; and 2) Melbourne has got to be raking it in off this ad. And the secret to what makes it so good isn't a secret; it's just rhyme.

How do I know this? Because sometimes people ask me, "Why don't you use rhyme?" My answer isn't defensive, but I tell them I use it a lot. And not just in sonnets, in free verse too. Take my poem "What Are Your Skills?" ("Poetry as Collage"). It rhymes, although maybe it would help a bit if I slowed down and highlighted where:

> Every year [at] Sea School
> we <u>were</u> taught [that] gla<u>ciers</u> <u>purr</u>

71

and ice /floes/, huge
be/low/ the s<u>ur</u>face, <u>were</u> sunning [cats].

<Call> ours a {failed} education.
If <u>it</u> makes you feel bett<u>er</u>,

<call> our hymns und<u>er</u> night skies
(cracked).

But for <u>thi</u>rteen years
we {sailed} on blu<u>er</u> wat<u>er</u>.

And <all> of us /know/ well
how to arch our (backs).

"But what if we'd rather have end rhyme sometimes so the poem sounds more like we expect it to?"

I don't disagree. Kids aren't the only ones who respond to rhyme and meter. I'm evidence of that myself. After hearing it a half a dozen times, I looked up Brady's "Far and Wide," the poem they'd taken those stanzas from for the commercial. It's in his book titled *Bells and Hobbles* (1911). It's got twelve more stanzas than the two in the ad, and I was right about poets and money; even Brady made his living from something other than his poetry—first as a clerk, and then as a journalist.

Anyway, I doubt this will get me any airtime in Melbourne, but here goes:

What would you do with a mini canoe?
And where would you keep it when you were through?

Would you shrink yourself down and find a big puddle
and paddle around way out in the middle?

Would you shrink yourself small to the size of a bee
and go to the tide pools at the edge of the sea

where the starfish and crabs will look larger than you?
What would you do with a mini canoe?

You could float in your alphabet soup, and each letter
would be so much bigger and taste so much better,

or float in the bath tub—as wide as the ocean—
and paddle real fast, or row in slow-motion.

These are just some of the things you can do
when you're mini enough for a mini canoe.

But where would you keep it when you were through
and changed back again to your own normal size
with your regular feet, hands, mouth, nose, and eyes?

Maybe you'd put it away in your pocket,
or into a drawer with a keyhole and lock it,

or up by your toothbrush next to the sink,
in the dish on the floor where the cat gets a drink,

or under your pillow so all night you'll dream
of the oceans you've been to, and the puddles, and streams.

A mini canoe can fit anywhere.
There's plenty of room up here, or down there.

But be sure to remember the place that you choose
because it's no fun to look for lost mini canoes.

NEW MYTHS AND ORIGIN STORIES

To tell a new story so true that it seems we've had it with us since the beginning—that's the goal when you're writing a new myth or new origin story. Or at least it's one of them.

I'm not sure I knew that—not so succinctly, anyway—until my brother Colin said so recently on the phone. He was talking about a reading I'd done on Zoom for the Utah Book Fest, specifically one poem and a short preface I'd shared to set it up, a preface I'd used at least a couple times over the years, but this was the first time he'd heard it. I talked for a minute about my life-long friend Jay Taylor. I said I'd called Jay up to see what he thought of some poems that I'd been working on, all of them beginning with the phrase "In the Old Songs about Washington." Our hometown, Puyallup, was pretty small when we were kids (unfortunately, it's all sprawl now), but it wasn't tiny like Enumclaw or Walla Walla. I mean, at least we had two high schools, one in the valley and one on the hill. Jay went to the one in the valley.

When I finished reading into the phone, Jay told me, "Man, I wish I would've gone to your school instead. We never learned any of that cool stuff."

"What cool stuff?" I asked him.

"Those stories, the Old Songs about Washington. All we ever studied was the boring parts."

"Well, we didn't study Old Songs either," I said. "They're brand new. I just made them up."

That was how I introduced the poem, and that's what struck my brother the most. Colin said, out of all the things I've written, "That's what's going to last, your origin stories about Washington. Even the people born here think they're true. You can't get more from an audience than that." And he's totally right.

Of course, your own origin stories don't have to be as place-specific. Most of mine aren't either. This one, for instance, is still connected to place but much more generally so:

WHAT ANY STONE CAN TELL YOU

When the earth discovered it was Earth, its astonishment became canyons, and its million years of laughter made them deep.

There, in those darker beds, it could lie down still and dream: dream waterfalls over granite, dream moss as soft as love, dream pines at impossible angles, strong as love. It dreamt animals across grasslands, animals into forests. It dreamt mountains to measure its distances, and birds to make sense of the sky.

But this wasn't enough; all things need another, even Earth.

And so do we. Not to own as if it were our echo. Not to give back less than we take. We are born—the earth's other—to our own astonishment; be grateful.

Be grateful, in Earth's arms, when your bones lie down at last to sleep.

Part of why I chose that example is because it behaves a little like a fable. It interrupts to make a statement, even to declare a kind of "moral to the story," but not so redundantly; I'm not summarizing something that's obvious to readers already, something they've already concluded themselves from the characters and actions. I'm just working on the imagery and diction some more, looking for the right kind of closure. If I wanted to tell people what to do, or turn the theme of the piece into explanatory prose, then I'd probably be better off writing those online homework study guides since they probably pay.

Bossing. Explaining. Writers should try not to do that, at least not in their final revisions. In the final revision, it's best to remember that readers know a lot too, and that they can sort out the heart-logic and head-logic themselves if we'll just stand aside and let them. Indirect characterization is better than direct characterization, or at least I think so.

Myths and origin stories are probably things you liked growing up, so why not try to write some? Listeners will recognize the form you're working in, but not the new information, so they'll want to stick around and hear how it all turns out. And that's all you're looking for: attention for the length of time you're asking to have their attention.

These two forms can help with that a lot. They're like a fire we've luckily inherited. All we've got to do now is add our own kindling and keep it lit.

ARCHITECTURE

I'm not an architect. Not unless you count reading *The Fountainhead* in high school, and you shouldn't. But poets do build things. Sometimes poorly, sometimes well, and I'm betting you know the difference. I'm betting you've read some poems that feel like waiting at the DMV (Department of Motor Vehicles), that crime against both patience and design with its purgatory furniture. Fluorescent lights. Linoleum. Dreary air. That sucks, and I hear you, but you've also known the opposite: poems that feel like going on a really great date, where the food and smells seem to come from God's own kitchen, and the wine is good, whether red or white and cold.

Or you've found the ones like a coffee shop—local and indie, not corporatized—where the tables might wobble a little, but the coffee isn't burned, and it doesn't come with sprinkles. Even if it's next to a vacuum store, the place feels somehow tucked away, a well-lit city oasis, with ceilings high enough to welcome in the wind if the doors are left open, and they are. And the music coming from the hidden speakers is exactly what you wanted, like E.S.P.—Simple Minds, or Talking Heads, or Bird since you can't go wrong with Charlie Parker. It's just what the doctor ordered, plus some chairs and exposed brick walls. You could stay here awhile, have another cup of coffee, take it in. That's what I'm talking about: poems half poem, half table-in-the-corner. Those are the kind I like trying to build, and maybe you'll think this is one:

> ### WHEN I WENT TO WORK AS A SNOW-GLOBE DESIGNER,
> I didn't do it for the usual reasons.
> I did it to get some practice in

before building my house at the bottom of the ocean.
Less traffic noise, for one thing,

and I've traded crows for manta rays. . .
a million fish like clouds

of colorful rain.
And my yard is a coral reef,

and I never shovel the sidewalk
since the snow just floats suspended in my dome.

You ought to come visit me. We could open some wine
and watch the sharks cruise over,

then sit together by the fireplace,
impossibly warm.

LOVE POEMS AS BUILT ENVIRONMENTS

In case there's a misperception out there, love poems aren't exactly easy. Writers can't sit around feeling until a love poem appears on the page like the King or Queen of Hearts—How nice would that be? But no. We haven't got access to a magic deck, and feelings—anyone's, a writer's included—are always a kaleidoscope blob of *non-verbal* until they shift, solidify, become words, and often not the right ones.

But that's the gig (or part of it), so here are three things that might help:

Suggestion 1
Start with the foundation—*What's your strength?*

For me, I think, it's to mythologize, so sometimes I've tried that. My wife Jen, for instance, is beautiful. And she has a sister, Hilary. So I thought about them as the characters in this:

> WHEN LIFE WAS BORN,
> so was her sister,
> and both of them were beautiful,
>
> so beautiful an eagle promised each
> a wing, one eye,
>
> and he gave Life half his heartbeats,
> gave her sister every other heartbeat;
>
> from then on, trying to fly from Death
> meant flying from himself, as well.

Nights he gathered the wolf pack's vision
and its long cascade of howls.

Days he collected the salmon's lunge upstream,
the salmon's memory.

These and more—two of everything—
the eagle brought to them as gifts,

and so both sisters loved him,
love all of us still.

What can we do, then, but hold Life tightly
and hold Death *just* as close?

Since Life is our sister,
Death is our sister.

All we can do, like salmon,
is know the ocean before returning home.

  Not a love poem, I know. But there *is* acceptance and discovery. Those
two things are a part of love, so there's that.

Suggestion 2
You need physics and math when you're building, and poems are a kind of
building, so—*Traditional forms won't cramp you. They can be tools.*
  Think about it, how many love poems did previous eras give us? I'd say,
"Lots." And a lot of them were sonnets:

.17 ACRES. CULINARY WATER
Not every decimal point is accurate.
They sometimes miss dimension, overlook

80

the sweep a peach tree adds to the backyard
just by moving in the wind. Imagine it

gone now, downed by a storm. Imagine books
with missing pages. . . you know it's more than words
that disappear. So don't discount the tree.
There's more to calculate than area.

Last summer, for instance, in the kitchen—peaches peeled,
the crust rolled out—who knows what she saw,
exactly, as I stood there making pie?

But she flashed a smile as bright as cinnamon,
and I could tell *exactly* what she meant.
Best one-point-something hours that whole July.

Suggestion 3
Still, I think what a lot of people want is a list of the loved one's qualities,
of the feelings those qualities create inside you, and they probably aren't
wrong to want that—*So try a list:*

To Jen
You are not the thunder in the story
though your heart does drum more deeply.

Not the lightning either
though you do know how to lash—

still fire in some memories.
No, you are the story of the story, the real:

how the folktale comes from Africa,
and you come from California,

and I come from somewhere
where the sun and words are rare—trees lost

in the fog, I guess, and words waiting
until they're driftwood,

and who will the people be that come along and climb,
hold hands and balance?

I heard once, and I haven't forgotten,
Whatever the weather is, it loves you.

And it's true: the shoreline lit up
or overcast, enough wind

to hear the chimes outside
or not, there's heat

or there isn't heat—
I feel it with you.

Until the snow comes blanketing.
Until what's left of me is just memories when it rains.

Now, that one's a love poem. I know it. The title, for example, is a give-away, and so is the end. But that doesn't make them weaknesses, just like doors and rooflines on a building aren't a weakness.

It's not weak to write for an audience. It isn't weak to tell someone what they mean to you. And writing—there's no way around it—takes giving, sometimes a little bit, and sometimes more.

The same as love.

SADNESS AS A NATURAL ENVIRONMENT

Years ago, I did a reading in a gallery. The owner wanted to keep the main lights off. She liked it better that way ("More atmosphere") and thought the cans in the ceiling and the spotlights on the art would be enough, and she was right. But it also meant some in the audience were more visible to me than others, and one of them had tears running down his face.

I hadn't expected that, although the poem I was reciting, "After the End," is definitely sad. How could it not be? It's about being extinct while you're still alive because if you're the last one left of your species, then there can't be any more; you're the end already. And in the meantime, you're also all alone.

I knew that was coming, but the man in the audience didn't, and it hit him hard.

Grief is like that. It gusts in fast, and it's unexpected. And sometimes when that happens, we say we're "at a loss for words." So it's probably a good thing that sad poems get written. They're places to keep the words for when someone need the words.

Still, sadness wasn't my intention with this next poem. Actually, when I started it, I didn't *have* intentions; I just like old-fashioned letterpress work. Where I went to college, Pacific Lutheran University, they have a studio devoted to book arts (The Elliott Press), and I got to take a class there: flat-bed Vandercook and treadle-wheel presses, dozens of typeface drawers, compositor sticks, handmade papers, a hellbox, you name it. So, yes, I knew about typesetting, but I didn't know who this typesetter was, and then a line popped into my head, and it caught me off guard: "He was a widower now, which he'd never imagined." Like loss just gusting in from nowhere.

I decided to follow that line and see where it would go:

THE TYPESETTER'S STORY
When he started in the typesetting business,
his hands were still new, not darkened from the ink yet.

And his eyes, which hadn't had to strain yet
sorting millions of letters into words,

could still see the ridge
and even tell the mountain goats from snow.

He was a widower now, which he'd never imagined:
her closet so permanently empty;

and around town, or coming through his doorway,
no one in her coat—not blue, more *azure* or *ocean*.

He always used that color for the title page,
never cut the folios clean,

and readers would find two pages
with no words at all.

Some wrote it off as a man's odd habit.
Others said, "The paper just got stuck."

But a few looked forward to those blank spots
as places to rest,

to let themselves drift awhile,
let the words so far roll back from wherever they'd come.

The typesetter had his own reasons, of course,
though he liked people saying, "They're a gift."

On one blank page, he thought about
how she'd fill it up with conversation.

And the other was the shape of her absence
each night in their bed.

Sadness wasn't my intention with this next one either, but current events stepped in and became the antagonist, and if the antagonist doesn't wind up losing in the end, what then?

The Story of the Girl

After the girl had thought of everything, she started again, keeping only the good thoughts this time, the ones she could share like snow from town to town, or like sun since it wasn't the weather that mattered.

But a man still got in a plane, and flew low, and shot 32 wolves from the air. And a woman ran for governor and won. Her message was that immigrants are evil.

So the girl tried again. She thought about her Nana, all the walks they used to go on, choosing sticks to strum some music from the chain-link fence, yet the president of Haiti was assassinated.

She thought about time—an open envelope—and each day a letter we were writing to the future. But still, someone painted swastikas downtown.

It wasn't working. Perhaps she needed to simplify: *As you've done it*, she thought, *unto the least of these*[1]—but no; a guy rammed his car through a Peace March.

Not all stories have a happy ending. Even less if the stories are true.

---

1   Excerpt from Matthew 25:40.

POETRY VS. BOOK BANS

People have always told stories. We've told them in order to find meaning, or create meaning, and then pass that meaning on to others (think myths, origin stories, and fables). We even did it visually before language evolved and got cookin' (think cave paintings).

But there have always been people who want to stop this seeking, finding, and passing on of meaning. There have always been people who want to censor it, ban it, burn it, or else co-opt it and use it as a self-serving tool for control and power.

We could even list this back-and-forth numerically if we wanted to: 1) The history of literature is our human story. 2) It's about finding or creating and passing on meaning, and doing so in a way that matters and therefore lasts. 3) This isn't easy in the first place or else everyone would be novelists and poets. 4) But it's even harder in a world where many—and many in power—think literature is a threat that needs silencing.

Which brings me to a story. It's a story about poetry, and it goes like this:

It was my dad who mentioned it. I had a poetry presentation coming up in Mr. Taylor's Advanced Placement English class, and my dad said, "You know, Mr. Taylor writes poems. I think a few of them are published," and that was that. I drove over to Pacific Lutheran University, asked a librarian the name of the school's literary journal, found the back issues in the stacks, checked the tables of contents, and the reward of finding Jim Taylor's poems that way beats the snot out of anything I've ever done by googling.

This was in 1986, so I can't remember the exact stanza breaks and lineation of his poems "Sequim Bay Summer" and "Lady on the Falls Church

Bus," but the lady was heavy, and this was the line about her sitting down: "The seat cushion gasps." That's three things all at once. That's personification, auditory imagery, and just plain cool, and the reason I knew any of this in 1986 was because Mr. Taylor taught me.

It's also why I remember the middle and ending of his poem "Sequim Bay Summer" to this day. Here is its vivid central image about fishing: "We catch bullheads uglier than stale sin." And here's what comes next, notching long-*A*, *K*, and *Uh* sounds together so rightly that the poem's music has stuck with me for 38 years: "The bay flattens and cools. Dusk ushers out the sun, the dock gut-slick from another day's aging." A lot of people can't pronounce the name "Sequim," or pronounce the name of the town where I went to high school either (Puyallup), but I bet they can re-read those lines three times and then recite them in the afterlife.

Oh, and my dad loved hearing about Mr. Taylor's reaction when I passed out copies of his poems and started my presentation not on Frost or Wordsworth or Sylvia Plath but on the work of a local poet published by Pacific Lutheran University. It was great. It was almost jack-in-the-box surprise, punctuated by, "Carney, you jerk," and "Where did you get these?!"

That was a good day. And days spent with literature, no matter who writes it, are good days still.

Why am I telling you this? Because, like me, you might be sick of all the loudmouth bullshit coming from the anti-literature crowd—sick of it up to the ceiling, to the attic, to the flight path of geese and the moon. I mean, it hurts my head just to wonder what they're thinking, so I won't. I'll just say this: Stories are a kind of light so we can see what's worth preserving. And poems are too.

I hope today, tomorrow, or next week a flock of good ones find their way to you.

IN THE BEGINNING WAS THE WORD

Despite the political time we're living in now, we can't let Habit and Lack of Imagination win. Habit thinks, "Brown skin shouldn't have a place here," and Lack of Imagination doesn't ask, "Why not?" Habit takes immigrants' kids away since, after all, it threatened to, and Lack of Imagination doesn't ask, "What the fuck?! And isn't that excessive for a misdemeanor?" No, it puts on a tie or a skirt-suit and tries to shift the blame. It lies about lying. In other words, it falls back on habit, and around and around.

You're damn right it's a vicious circle.

So what can a poem do about it? Call it out, talk back, be the opposite, I guess. Remind us *In the beginning was the Word*, then try to use the best ones. That's what King David was up to, I think, not knowing he'd be quoted for three thousand years. Saint Paul didn't know he'd be a saint and that his letters would last for two millennia. And Walt Whitman? When Whitman spoke to the future, he was speaking to hope. It wasn't a given that we'd hear him; it was just a belief. All of them: writers.

So what's the best way?

How should I know? You ought to see the tumbleweed scribble I produce just looking for some sort of forward direction. Still, I do believe—if I had to pick some basics—that writing well comes down to these four things:

First, poems should be more than ornamental; they should try to be useful. Others have said it a bit differently—the Utah poet Ken Brewer, for instance, said that poems should "offer a name for something in the shadows of our lives"—but they mean the same thing: Poems have jobs. They use the five senses to get at the essential.

Second, we need new myths, fables, and origin stories. These old forms were magnetic and primal and still are. People might think they've heard them all before and *Yeah yeah, I know,* but they haven't heard ours yet. To ours, they might still listen. They'll recognize the old form but not the new information, so they'll let themselves sit still to learn the ending. Here's what I mean:

SOMETIMES IT ISN'T THE SAME OLD STORY

You could understand him misunderstanding,
digging such careful holes with his shovel,

sifting in spoonfuls of birdseed—
an honest mistake.

And you could half-understand how he stubbornly finished,
how he aimed his back at everyone laughing

and patted the dirt down
gently with his hands.

But to greet each day with his watering can,
to go on as if he were a gardener, as if he *believed*. . .

someone finally stomped all the green in his yard,
and that should've been the end of that.

Certainty feels like a flag when you fly it.
It snaps in the wind

and makes the sound of your own good name,
of your own high opinion. It's the opposite of birds.

And it was birds that he was growing, after all:
cardinals, robins, chickadees, starlings.

His seedlings stood up again,
unfurled their branches,

all of them loaded not with blossoms but with song.
That was the season people re-learned amazement,

followed by the autumn when they re-learned amazement again:
One morning he went 'round his yard on a ladder,

he paid no attention to everyone clapping,
just picked each bird and released it into the sky.

Third, it isn't just myths that help us to know the unknowable. Other kinds of poems can do that too. The key is to ground them in concrete details we can care about or argue with. I heard the poet Marvin Bell say once, "I like poems whose ideas have their feet in the dirt." Me too.

And fourth, poems should create a vivid moment. And the secret to doing that is action. Meaning, verbs rather than adjectives; meaning, put most of your adjectives in the interrogation chair and ask, "What do you think you're doing here?" Besides, verbs are more descriptive anyway. They zing, groan, stagger, steam, and zip. Verbs can pogo, while an adjective just has a big happy smile while it jumps.

And that's that—four things for your tool box. Put them together with your heart, and build the world a better vision. Writers always have.

III.

SEVEN RIVERS

"FOR YOUR ESSAY, DESCRIBE SEVEN RIVERS"

1.

I only know one river with a serial killer named after it: the Green River. The bodies of murdered women kept getting found along its banks.

This wasn't your Green River, not unless you're from Washington state and your formative years were the 1980s. Your Green River—whether in British Columbia or South Africa or a dozen other places—might be very nice. Ours was an ongoing nightmare on the local news.

Yet that's where we went to go inner-tubing or cliff jumping, me and Jay and Brian. Our own town's river, the Puyallup, was a concrete channel, a straight and muddy *nothing* routed west to the Port of Tacoma. Green River was blue, and it wasn't a long drive to get there: Get off the highway in Auburn, then it's 15 miles, maybe less, unless we missed a turn.

2.

Which admittedly we did sometimes since we were 16 and more focused on the stereo. Adam and the Ants? Maybe. Rush again? Most likely; Rush was Brian's constant, and it was probably his Datsun we were riding in. Sometimes the grunge band, Green River? Definitely not; they were local, but none of us had heard of them, and that word and genre—*Grunge*—hadn't been coined yet. That would come later, screaming out of Aberdeen, a place we never even thought about unless we were headed for Ocean Shores, and we never were. No girls in bikinis like the Promised Land of California, just cold, and wind, and a couple miles of sand dunes, a lot of them with fire pits full of burned up Rainier Beer cans. Plus, the last two towns before getting there, Aberdeen and Grays Harbor, were bleak as hell from the timber mills closing. Not for us.

Green River was ninety minutes closer, and we figured all the evil was contained in our parents' TVs.

3.

This isn't the part where I tell you that we stumbled on a body, or that one of those women was anyone we knew or a girl from our high schools. And I'm not going to tell you what the killer did either. That's some psychopathic shit that no one needs to hear. I'm saying we were kids; we're in our fifties now, so you know there's no real danger. The three of us, we drifted through just fine.

4.

Not everyone did, of course. One time a man did drown, and our moms made sure to tell us when we got home. There'd been news on the radio.

"Did you know they opened up the floodgates this morning?"

There are floodgates?

"Couldn't you tell that the river was faster?"

Sure, plus an eight-foot waterfall where there'd never been a waterfall.

"Why do something so dangerous?"

Because it's fun.

5.

Maybe it's like that with everything, at least when you think about it later: so many details flowing around, and more things mixed in than we can ever know. We just float along on the present moment. Look up at the sunlight sometimes. Watch out for downed trees stabbing in from the riverbanks, roots-first. Try not to flip off our tubes or get a boulder up our asses. That sort of thing.

And maybe that's what stories are for: to remember the *actual*, to fish it out of the *historical*, to find our own selves and say hello again, and say hello to you, the reader.

6.

If so, then stories are a lot like water. Which is good, although water can drown us. Which is good, although everything in Utah is drying up and the Great Salt Lake is just a few years from extinction.

Still—maybe even because of this—our stories are a lot like water.

Someone's thirsty? A poem can be water.

Someone's drowning and she wouldn't mind a goddamn rope? A story can be a rope if the story is right.

7.

And that's how it's always been. The Anasazi people, for instance—they lived here a thousand years before me—here (most likely) for the rivers, and then gone (most likely) when the rivers dried up. And what did they leave behind for us? Their art, their petroglyph narratives.

These petroglyphs aren't legalese. They aren't reports of another murder. No, they're better than that, and they're clearly for *something*. Like a river, people carved them into rock. Like a river, people painted them on canyon walls. So I know this isn't a proper conclusion, but maybe that's okay:

WHY WE HAVE ART
Because no one put away the easel,
our yard filled up with paintings, the sunlight

waking each morning to something new, unsigned,
a welcome mystery.

We strung them like prayer flags—such color
hanging from our porch eaves—then took them

and mounted them on tree trunks
all along the block.

"It must be the ghost," a few said,
"of that old guy who always had a sketch book."

"It's a democrat plot." "It's an angel."
But nobody cared; no one got sleuthy about it.

Mostly our street felt lucky for once: to be picked
and visited by wonder. Like rain

if you could set a frame around it.
Like the sound of *no-sound* when it snows.

CIVICS LESSONS

1.

What happened isn't always interesting. Not compared to what didn't.

For instance, decades ago it was decided that the study of government would be called Civics. Not Principles of Design, not Wisdom Forensics, not What Sort of Citizens Elected This Wizard? Those other names got passed over, and it's too bad because learning about acoustics instead of political noise, or the rightness and function of an arch compared to the U.S. Electoral College might have made this a country where the fish aren't so full of mercury.

2.

Thirty-four years ago, I crashed my parents' car. It was dark, almost midnight—even everyone's porch light asleep—and the place my parents had moved was new to me: Fox Island, Washington.

Maybe without the fog, or if the roads had been straighter, but they weren't; they were more like a grandma's cursive, and the fog was thick enough to win some kind of award. Add black ice, and the dome light on and me reading a list of directions, then a curve into yet another down slope, this one into T-intersection, and I only had a second to wonder *Who put a hill in the middle of the road?* and then *bam*.

That's what happened. *The actual.*

3.

But I can't help thinking about the stories that didn't, all the ones less fogged in by facts. Like a next-day story at the salvage yard, maybe, a story about the tow-truck driver who'd gotten the call. Maybe he noticed my things—a couple books, a yellow notepad—flung on the floor in front of the passenger seat, so he borrowed some paper, wrote a note, and attached it to the bill—

4.

Dear Driver,

Good news is, since you're reading this, you're alive. Bad news is it's time to shop for a car. Judging from the windshield, you're going to want to wait though—perfect impression of your forehead, and blood sort of spiderwebbing in the cracks. Some of your hair there too, a couple strands of it. Car shopping sucks without a headache thrown in the bargain. Speaking of bargains, these guys here won't be giving you one. What they'll offer you, tops, is two-fifty. That's their impound fee, plus my towing, plus another $50 bucks to buy the deed. Got to have the deed before they part it out. I know a yard that'll maybe go $400.00. I'd've taken your car there in the first place, but the Sheriff said "Tow it to the nearest" etc. Anyway, my number's on the bill if you want to call. From your books, I see you're a Lutheran. Pacific Lutheran University Library. I don't still go to Mass much but keep a rosary hanging from my rear-view mirror. Said an "Our Father" for you last night and hope that you're o.k. On a more practical note—and believe me, you're going to want to do this—get all that broken glass in your head out now. Every single sliver. If there's pieces of glass still in there, well, when they start to work their way to the surface you'll have to slice the scars open with an X-acto knife and tweezer around in the infection. Here's the part where I tell you "Wear a seatbelt" like I'm some kind of too-late Guardian Angel. Sincerely, James "Mac" McIntyre. P.S.: I hope you don't think that the Lutheran stuff was me being a jackass criticizing. Just thought you might like knowing about the prayer.

5.

That's what I mean about what *didn't* happen. What could have is the better, more necessary story.

6.

And here's a third example, this one out of *The Salt Lake Tribune* (A6, 3 March 2016):

What Happened:

This senator, Todd Weiler (Republican), got ticked off about members of the Navajo Nation seeking to re-name Columbus Day. During debate on their petition—standing on the floor of the Senate—he said, "The native population gave the early explorers syphilis, which they brought back to Europe. Blaming Columbus for the extermination of the native population is as fair as blaming the native population for people who die using tobacco and cocaine, which the natives introduced to the Europeans."

7.

What Didn't Happen:

He wasn't wearing a Pharaoh outfit. Frogs didn't rain from the Senate ceiling. No one had to hopscotch over bright green insights to take a seat, vote *No*, and kill their bill.

I HAVEN'T FINISHED THIS ESSAY YET, AND ALREADY IT'S ILLEGAL IN FLORIDA

Subvert the dominant paradigm!

That's a phrase I read once and haven't ever forgotten. Was it written somewhere across a chalkboard? Graffiti-ed on a boxcar? Painted on one of those homemade banners people sometimes drape along an overpass? I'm not sure. I don't remember the *where*, but I can't forget the words.

Probably the reason I remember them is because they feel like my own M.O. when it comes to writing. For one thing, I think paradigms are camped out on the boring side. For another, the phrase reminds me that my writing ought to have a purpose, that being decorative or entertaining isn't enough. And third, it's a way to avoid redundancy because writing takes work, and it isn't easy, so writing about what's already been written—supporting the established and cemented—well, to me, that seems like a waste of effort and time.

Take origin stories, for instance. Whether the go-to source is Genesis or Ancient Greek mythology, the plot is the same. And worse, the point of these two sources was to blame all our problems on women, then set up our social systems on the questionable premise that women can't be trusted with decision-making.

If you're someone who's served by such a premise and you'd rather have men be exclusively in charge, then that's a neat trick, but it's awfully self-serving. And it isn't a very good origin story either, not if you want stories to be interesting. So instead, when I decided to write my own, I started with two simple changes: Instead of Eden, I set mine in Washington state; and instead of Adam coming first, I flipped things around made *that* the origin story's title:

In the Beginning Was a Girl

In the Old Songs about Washington, a girl woke up
with feathers instead of hair, woke up with silver eyes

and saw behind the moon, which was where the Future
tried to hide Himself 'til it was time.

The Future liked His secrets,
lifting each one up like an oyster,

sometimes breaking one open to put in a pearl,
sometimes to swallow it whole,

and in the Old Songs this meant the girl possessed a power,
and that she'd be tempted:

offered necklaces of moonstones, dresses of spun moonlight,
the wild permission of wolf packs to run with them and hunt,

anything the Future could think of to trade,
to get back His secrecy. But she refused.

What she wanted was a moment, a single piece of Him
to press against her skin, to hold and grow in her body,

and that was all. The Future agreed to this bargain.
Which is how, according to the Old Songs, we were born.

Or take Langston Hughes' poem "Theme for English B." The speaker is braver and smarter than the essay topic assigned to him. And he's so reflective about differences and samenesses that I want this poem to be "true"; as in, factual. I want it to be what Langston Hughes turned in to his professor. It's got a voice that's the opposite of boring. It's both purposeful and well-written. And it isn't ever redundant no matter how often I read it. I would've just thought, "Wow," and given his poem an A.

What about the state of Florida, though? What grade would *it* slap down? Not even an F, just a make-believe "Missing"; and, therefore, a score of zero.

Florida has enacted laws against the existence of poems like "Theme for English B," as if it can legislate everyone's eyes closed, order that they un-eat apples, lock understanding of others in Pandora's Box, and then feel dominant and smug. As if it wants to yank out all our question marks and then chuck them in a landfill: "Oh, brave new world [exactly like the world that we'd prefer]."

Me, I prefer Wallace Stevens. I prefer what he wrote in the final section of his poem "Six Significant Landscapes":

> Rationalists, wearing square hats,
> Think, in square rooms,
> Looking at the floor,
> Looking at the ceiling.
> They confine themselves
> To right-angled triangles.
> If they tried rhomboids,
> Cones, waving lines, ellipses—
> As, for example, the ellipse of the half-moon—
> Rationalists would wear sombreros.

Of course, those lines aren't an exact match for what I mean. To be exact, they would need to say "*ir*rationalists" because banning books, and criminalizing curriculum, and requiring that teachers teach the upsides of slavery—none of these things are rational at all. There's no human reasoning there.

Dominance, yes. A faulty paradigm, yes. But something we can say *Amen* to?

Absolutely no.

FOUR FACTS

Over the years, I've heard some interesting facts: that the Baja Peninsula will one day be an island, that raccoons wash their hands more than we do, that if pigeons don't roost along an overpass, then its structural integrity can't be insured without an indemnity clause. I've heard the Visigoths are why we have Christmas trees. I've heard that kangaroos are ambidextrous. And none of these facts are worth checking, so I don't. I just agree that they're interesting.

So now, in that same spirit, I thought you might like this handful:

Fact 1: The Earth Isn't Flat
Once, on an overnight flight headed east, I actually saw the Earth's curve, saw the sunrise trace it with an arc of light. But I was tired, not ready to wake up yet, so I turned from the window and just went back to sleep.

And one time on the train from Spokane to Tacoma, I woke up to all of these passengers talking. It was clear that they were all from faraway places, that this was their first trip to Washington, and we were winding through the Cascade Mountains, and it was dawn—so enough light to see by—and the people kept saying, "Can you believe it? Look at all the trees. This can't be real. There's too many."

And another time, I was driving home from L.A. It was the end of my freshman year, and I wasn't going back: a packed car, a late start leaving, too young and too cheap to split the drive in two and sleep in a motel, so I was pretty wiped out by the time I got to the Siskiyous.

Coffee, I'd heard, can wake you up, so I stopped in Grants Pass and got a booth at a Denny's. My plan was to drink a whole pot, top to bottom, and drink it black so I'd learn to like the taste by the end and not spend my whole life stirring milk and sugar. And I did make it home, and I still drink it black, so there's that.

But what do these memories have in common?

I don't know, except that there's some traveling in them. That's probably why I've been thinking about it—writing is kind of a journey with horizons too. And an arc. And a meeting somewhere in the middle. Logically, there has to be: Writing is only one origin point. Reading is the other. And what we call The Story happens in between.

Fact 2: Why We Have Fire

The sky was the sky, and beautiful, but lonely. In its endless heart, what it wanted was a hawk. Each day it listened for the hawk's fierce screaming, and nights it carried the moon like a lantern, keeping watch, but nothing happened. It sent rain, sent wind, and still nothing. No hawk rose suddenly below.

If you miss a man until missing him feels wide as the horizon, or love a woman from a distance, you'll understand.

But know this too: Finally the sky tore its longing into lightning, bursting open an oak, and that flash became the hawk's eyes, and its wings and its pride and its hunger. . . just a flash, then the First Hawk rising, bringing fire.

Fire to guide us. To be our comfort, our fury, our desire.

Fact 3: Air Is for Breathing, and for Mythic Birds

Apparently—I heard this once—Benjamin Franklin didn't want the eagle for our national bird. He wanted the turkey instead. In school, we're taught that he was smart—that all the Founding Fathers were—but this was dumb. I mean, the *turkey*? What the hell?

And symbols do matter. Look at sports: the Kentucky Wildcats, Arizona Wildcats, Villanova Wildcats, Kansas State Wildcats; the Nevada Wolf Pack, North Carolina State Wolfpack, Michigan Wolverines; and so on. Although, sure, there are also some outliers—the *un*-fierce, the odd, the improbable—like the Oregon Ducks; they call themselves "The Quack Attack." But mostly the Ducks sucked at sports until they got rich from all of that Nike money. Disney made a movie called *The Mighty Ducks* since even little kids like irony, since an underdog story with a couple of laughs is okay, but it isn't a national bird. And neither is an idiotic turkey.

No, for that you go with a raptor, an eagle. Eagles are better because they seem worthy of myths.

Fact 4: The Person You Love Is 72.8% Water
> I don't know if I'm going to hell,
> but I like toast for breakfast,
>
> and I can eat breakfast
> any time of day.
>
> A woman's slender arms
> make me wish I was a painter.
>
> Cats belong in every bookstore. They'll make the words
> seep deeper in your bones.
>
> If God and I were on a rocky beach,
> we'd search out perfect skipping stones.
>
> I'd tell Him my favorite miracle:
> water into wine.
>
> My favorite mood is Angry. That's a lie.
> My favorite sin is lying. That's not true,
>
> but it dresses up the story
> like a good storm dresses up the sky,

like fire and fiddles take wood and make it speak.
I know, I know—water isn't wine.

But at night, when someone's thirsty,
you can bring it, cold as heaven. They can drink.

ONE FORECAST: FIRE

No one can talk about summer anymore without also talking about fire. It's the common denominator. Europe, Africa, Australia, North America—fire, like disaster cartography. It's too huge for the news to put a frame around, yet they have to try. I mean, this has to be reported.

What happens, though, if the citizens don't listen? What happens if the ones they vote for listen even less?

I don't want to wait for an answer, and stories—I believe this is true; I've seen it happen—stories can zoom in on details that help us understand. They help us to *experience* and, therefore, care, and caring might lead to action.

It seems worth trying, anyway. If the old results are both bad and predictable, then maybe setting, character, and plot can reach more people than facts can. Or just help the facts have an impact when the news turns to fire:

"Break a Leg, and They Put You Out to Pasture"
"Take everything you don't know, line it up, you've got the horizon. But get your head in a book, you've got a boat."

That's the kind of thing he'll say between two bites of an apple. It's one of the reasons I don't mind him crossing the street when I'm watering the yard. He's earned these analogies: worked 23 years as a fire jumper, wound up with seven breaks in his ankle and leg, a whole scaffolding of steel inside.

Another reason is the cider he brings me: "Easiest way to deal with the apples." He says, "I ought to just burn the damn tree, but I'm too used to putting fires out."

≈

"Maybe not a boat, exactly. But an oar, for sure. Or a spyglass."

By now he's wielding the hose while I follow and watch, fake professional interest. He's spraying at the bees around the flowers like he's putting out sparks. He's probably right about the spyglass: You open a book and draw the distance nearer, the words inside it help clarify, and it's all done with mirrors, by reflection. Not a bad trick.

It makes me wonder sometimes if a tree he saved became paper, or a hundred board feet of pencils, or a chair in a bookstore café.

≈

I imagine the heat, of course—everywhere-pressing and heavy as water— but the roar of standing in a world of fire, not a pulsing and pausing like the shoreline's heartbeat, a constant sound swallowing all sound, that's harder to do.

And thirst. I half forgot about thirst: all those back-to-back shifts drinking nothing but smoke.

"I could've retired," he says. "No one expects more than twenty. But it felt like jumping into empty air and then landing with nothing to do."

The hose is rolled up by the side of the house now, the whole yard shining from sunlight on water, and we're standing on the porch, drinking cider, talking about raccoons. They're his only regret, he tells me. Not the leg; he's seen tree trunks more shattered. Four baby raccoons, maybe five months old. He saw the flames reflecting off their eyes, pulled them out of a hollow, shoved them in his coat, got them down to the base camp, poured iodine onto the bite marks and scratches, went back in.

He found out the next morning.

"They just took 'em to the county pound and put 'em to sleep."

≈

There's a field I pass by on my way to work so out of place in the landscape—too close to new tract homes and cul-de-sacs, shopping, a thousand miles from Texas, a hitch in the step, a break in the usual line—where they're grazing all these longhorn cows.

I love that part of the drive. I don't belong here either. My neighbor and I, we've got that in common, enough that we never have to talk about it, enough we just wave in the winter while shoveling snow, unburying sidewalks. It's how I know that he really will burn that tree, yell out at me to come on over.

He'll hand me a last jar of cider, then stand there, probably with pain in his leg. And I'll stand there too and help him watch the fire.

SIX TRIBUTES

1.

There's this moment when you're northbound on the interstate to Seattle where you round a bend and see both the Smith Tower (old-style, and not what you'd think of as a high-rise) and the Columbia Tower too, looming over it (black glass, and absolutely a skyscraper). You can also see Elliott Bay and the Olympic Mountains. It's an iconic blend of the built and the natural, at least to me.

The Smith Tower was once Seattle's tallest building, the tallest, in fact, west of the Mississippi. So when a taller one went up somewhere, Seattle added a kind of spire to the top in order to regain the lead—sort of like an architectural flip-off raised with style.

Anyway, seeing the two buildings together—Smith and Columbia—seeing that early- and late-20th-century contrast, is pretty incredible. And none of it would be possible without welders. There's a skeleton in each of those buildings. And the people who made sure all those bones and girders stood up and kept on standing—despite wind, and rain, and the steepness of the hillside, and time, and earthquakes, and proximity to four volcanos—the people who made sure they kept on standing were the working-class laborers with their welding torches.

April is National Welding Month, a good time to thank them for the skyline and share a poem:

THE WELDER'S STORY
No surprise he likes the odd jobs best.
Like fixing the crack in the church bell.

He'd never been up in a belfry before,
or braided his work between pigeons,

and now each noon
he listens 'til the echoes end.

Or the windows in submarines;
those portholes need to seal tight.

And that stealth job, museum guy,
knight's armor, total panic:

He'd snuck it out for Halloween, then fell
and snapped off the nose-piece thing.

Now, repairs like that—both Medieval
and invisible—that's art.

Also, if anyone needs it,
he'll weld moonlight to the harbor. . .

a place to go when you're fractured,
split by grief.

Row out, work quietly, blue sparks
past the end of the pier.

He can do it so the breaks seem hardly there at all.

2.
World Whale Day is the third Sunday in February. I can't be the only one
who thinks this isn't enough, that this is absurd. Just one out of 365 days?

A single calendar box? That's the best we can manage for the humpbacks and bowheads and grays? I mean, what are we even doing here?

This poem won't add another day for them, I know. But I'm offering it anyway so that maybe throughout the year's shortest month, we'll remember to think about whales.

THE SUBMARINER'S STORY

For starters, you say it "subma*reen*er,"
not the English way. Like what,

just because they had Shakespeare
now it's, "Al-you-mini-oom biscuit save the Queen?"...

not as long as *she's* the captain. And second,
and this is what matters: Think like a whale:

All the fathoms and distance.
All the seafloor mountains snowless.

All the cuttlefish shifting
like kaleidoscopes of light,

these lightshows with poisonous beaks,
these beaks that'll cut through crabs.

All this blue, where all sounds elongate, is your home.
So there's nothing to miss here.

That's something the whales know already, of course,
and one day the linguists will prove it.

They'll translate their singing,
and the chorus will be, "It's our home."

3.

At the post office, the clerk wanted to know, "Do you write books?" I had a bunch of padded envelopes addressed to different bookstores, and I told him yes.

"About what?" he asked.

And there it was: that moment when I wasn't quite sure what to tell him because one book includes some orca linguistics and the worst-ever firestorm in Spokane, and another is a shark mythology, and another starts out with a time-traveling revenge tale and ends with an elegy set in Northern California, and the one I had with me—the one that I was mailing—covers even more ground than that.

I said, "Mostly about the West, I guess. About animals and the environment. Poems and essays, not novels," and the clerk said, "Oh."

That's the way it goes, I know. But I could've been even more disappointing. Imagine if I'd told him, "Lately, I've been writing new parables," what then? A look of confusion. A headshake.

Still, there's just something about the parable form that I like. I like the way it's both sideways and urgent, and your thoughts disappear into one-minute stories, here-and-gone, but maybe still hanging in the air like they're gusts and the reader is a wind chime. I think this century could use some new parables, and maybe you think so too:

THE STORY OF THE MERMAIDS

When the mermaids filed a class-action lawsuit, some thought they didn't have standing. Another thought maybe they did, but only on a boat: "You know, because of Maritime Law."

She said, "That means all we have to do is bore a few holes in the ones at the marina. I know sinking boats sounds expensive, but believe me, not compared to punitive damages."

She meant owing for the decades and miles of lost nets, adrift now and noosing through the water. She meant for oil spills and barges of garbage a century deep. She meant for kelp beds the size of the Amazon gone, and everything coastal with them, from rockfish and otters and abalone, to the ocean's biggest carbon sink, to mermaids complaining that our plastic is worse than disease.

There was a pause. Waves sloshed against the pilings. Then somebody spoke.

"On the other hand," he reminded them, "mermaids aren't even people, so the judge'll toss this out, and we're off the hook."

And it sounded like wisdom, and everyone cheered.

4.

There's a line in a poem by Tomaz Salamun where he says, "one day I thought who'll be the first one to count up to a million." I love that. I dig it because it's both weird and reassuring. It tells me that the pinball thoughts in my own head aren't so weird after all.

Like this one, for instance: Does there have to be a sacred point for a story to be a parable?

And also this one: Do people really *exalt* and *vow obedience* to technology, or is this just a recent kind of deus-ex-machina thinking? Should I have a séance and contact Aristotle and ask him, or would doing that be pointless since I can't speak Ancient Greek, so now it's me and a bearded vapor-guy trying to communicate by pantomime, when the phone rings again, and it's the Awareness Association constantly haranguing me for money, and Aristotle's pointing at the thing in my hand and running through a series of faces, and believe me, I get it; it's a phone and he's never seen one; but he just looks strange: sort of wide-eyed, followed by forehead-scrunchy, with his lips together in an *O*-shape slid to the right—*This guy's a philosopher?! Holy-Moly*—what is he, curious, flirting, scientifically interested, disgusted by a world chock-full of beeping interruptions, asking for the bathroom, asking for a milkshake, *what?* Or maybe he wants me to tell them, "Sorry, Aristotle isn't home."

So anyway, no, a parable doesn't have to have a sacred point. It just has to be narrative, constructed from a metaphor, with people instead of animals as characters, and short:

BEFORE ANYONE WAS EVEN FINISHED,
the day began again, like the sky had hit rewind. So the people poured more cereal and took another shower.

Then it kept on happening, the day jumping back to start over, people's cars going *Zwip!* in the middle of their commutes.

It was pretty ridiculous. A woman said, "Someone should fix this." So a team of physicists was summoned; plus, a Strong Man arrived.

"Tie this rope to that mountain," one said.

"Our equations will prove," said the others.

"Now everyone yell *Pull!* and I'll pull the other way."

"Quark wormhole. Quark wormhole."

Both of these were great ideas, but neither worked—just some boredom and a couple torn hamstrings, just news vans with cables and cameras and little to report. Except rent beyond the reach of most incomes now. And laws taking voting from the voters now. And heat domes over Antarctica now.

"We oughtta shoot a nuke at the sun," a man said, "or else troll it on the inter—"

But before he could finish his thought, the day began again.

5.
I'm not going to fake it here and say each year isn't full of terrible news. It is.

But each year ends with the holidays too; as in, *holy* and also *plural*; meaning, we get a whole season of days to focus, instead, on what's meaningful and possible.

Hopefully this next one helps to point in that direction:

THE STORY OF THE TOWNSPEOPLE
Because no one could think of where they put it, the whole town had to pitch in. Yes, it was really annoying, but everyone tried, calling out across fences and such.

"Anyone check in the couch cushions yet?"

"Did you look by the clock in the kitchen?"

"How 'bout on the mantel?"

"We don't have a mantel."

"One time, I found my keys in the freezer."

"Me too," a man said, "but it wasn't there."

It might have helped to know what they were searching for. Some thought it must be concern for others since they hadn't seen much of that lately. Others figured justice needed finding. Others mercy, but they couldn't be sure.[1]

In the meantime, neighborhoods got straightened up a little, and a dog who'd been stuck in a basement was found and taken home: so hungry, so *happy-after-lonely*.

"Well. . ." a man said, and "That's right," a woman answered, "we'll meet here and do this tomorrow."

Not a plan, exactly. More humble than that. But things keep turning up the more they look around.

6.

I've never heard anyone say they think that origin stories are boring. Probably because as toddlers we always asked *why?* Jen and I have a grand-daughter, Rhyan, and she can repeat it all day: "But why?"

"You should put on your shoes before we go outside."

"But why?"

"Because the grass has a lot of pine needles in it."

"But why?"

"Because they fall off the tree, and they're pointy and sharp."

"But why?"

"Well, it's sort of like our hair. Sometimes our hair falls out, and some-times pine needles fall out too, to make room for new ones."

"But why?"

"Because a long time ago, the very first tree felt sad that she was alone. She felt sad, and she started to cry, only she couldn't make tears the way that people do—"

---

1   Adapted from Micah 6:8.

"But why?"

"Because trees don't have eyes, just branches, so what rolled down her cheeks were pine cones and needles, but that was good because—"

"But why?"

"Because they landed on the ground and then grew into other trees. Like a family. And from then on the first tree knew she wasn't alone."

"Okay, Papa, I wear shoes now."

And we went outside.

Were there other ways off of this toddler merry-go-round? Not really. I guess there's the old standby *because I said so*, but wielding that gavel comes with downsides, and anyway, I prefer an origin story. The world's stuffed full of destruction already, so any chance to focus on the opposite, any chance to focus on creation, might be a gift. Like our daughter, Alabama, is a gift. And so is her daughter, Rhyan.

IV.

RACCOON VERSES

SPELLING

I was a spelling tutor once for three Arab guys—Mohammed, Muhammed, and Khalid. We'd meet and I'd agree that it's a pitchfork curse, that *zoo*, *blue*, *shoe*, *through*, *view* and *two* shouldn't rhyme; that *heart* with *part*, and *haunt* with *want*, and *reign* with *brain* were insane—and then we'd go shoot pool.

Muhammed was the best at it, an extrovert, always smiling, so on the day he said he didn't want to, I could tell that he was feeling down.

"I miss camels," he said. "Here there are only cows."

To hell with idioms. He'd hit on a better way to say, "I'm homesick." And right now, sitting in my house, I'm homesick too. Not for camels, for water.

Astrology tells me there's a reason for this. My zodiac sign is the Crab, and I'm landlocked. Four-thousand feet above sea level. Utah.

But just like with spelling—an *e* on the end makes the vowel sound long, but not in the case of the number "one"—there must be exceptions. I mean, somewhere there's bound to be a Taurus (Earth sign) who totally lives to water ski, or a Virgo (another Earth sign) who up and buys a kayak in her thirties, turns herself halfway into an otter, even inventing new coves in her sleep, and new woods with accessible places to launch from. One night she finds her arms moving under the blankets, enough that she wakes herself up: It's the middle of the night, it's her bedroom, and the nearly fluid sunlight cutting through the overcast was just a dream. The sound of her paddle dipping, dipping, dipping in the lake was just rain outside getting scooped at her house by wind gusts. The weather and her limbs tuned and rhythmic. Liquid whispers.

Water: Mix it with grain and time, you get whiskey; with pigment and talent, you get art; with salt, and now you have a home for orcas. Mix it with imagining and memory, and I don't feel quite so homesick anymore.

How do you spell "kayaker"? W-a-t-e-r.

How do you spell "hypnotic"? W-a-t-e-r.

How do you spell "want" and "heart" and "rain"? W-a-t-e-r.

LINGUISTICS

Salt Lake City

I made a quick stop at *7-11* this morning to grab what, a Kind Bar? a Power Bar?—oh, marketing, you're so ridiculous—and a second cup of coffee, and at the register I said, "This is a re-fill," and the clerk said, "Use the app, honey, so it's free," and I said, "I don't have a phone," and she said sorry and rang me up the extra dollar. Not sorry that I don't own a cell phone; it was way too early to get existential. She meant that she wished she didn't have to charge me.

I didn't mind paying, but there are two things now that I'm wondering: First, do people really put up with spam and corporate tracking in exchange for a cup of coffee? And second, would my kid look over my shoulder at this and tell me, "That's a lot of *and*s in that paragraph, Dad"? His teacher, I guess, has a rule against it.

The problem isn't all the ands, though. It's the word "app," which isn't actually a word so much as a tone-deaf, lame abbreviation. And it isn't alone. It's got company—"twitter," "tweet," and "hashtag," for instance. Linguists would call them neologisms, but they're the worst, "hashtag" especially. "Hashtag" is the rake you step on so your face gets cartoon handle-smacked. Ever try *uni* (raw sea urchin)? That stuff is hashtag. It tastes like the tide flats, can't be swallowed, doesn't chew. It just amoebas around in your mouth and won't go down, like a dog-slobbered racquetball. It's got to be the dumbest word ever, and there isn't an app to get rid of it.

No, our only recourse is to stay on the side of aesthetics and memory, and since this all started with coffee, here are two memories about that— the first one set in Spokane and the other one in Ireland.

Spokane, Washington

The all-at-once-everywhere espresso bug originated in Seattle, but it didn't take long before it spread across the state. It crossed a mountain range, range lands, the Columbia River, miles and miles of wheat fields, and *shazam!*—cappuccino kiosks appearing overnight, one of them a hundred yards from where I lived (South 608 Stevens, the Altadena Apartments, just down the hill from St. John's Cathedral). Two young women were running it, both of them mythically beautiful. I unplugged and shoved aside my coffee maker. It seemed like the right thing to do.

But it didn't last. Each double latte cost more than a pint, and I could do the math. Pretty baristas have their upside, but beer is beer.

Ireland

A year later, mid-summer, I was billeted in Dublin. That's their word for it, "billeted"; meaning, something less than a boarder but more than passing through. Anyway, each night our host asked us (my friend Tod was there too; we were students), "What would you like for breakfast tomorrow?" and I'd say, "Coffee, please, if you have it," and each morning she'd bring out eggs, blood pudding, pots of tea.

Good tea. Tea I could really get used to.

In fact, I even got insistent about it one weekend out in Sligo. Tod and I had gone there for a music festival, and maybe to check out Innisfree, but first—this was Tod's idea—we needed to climb Queen Mab's burial mound.

It wasn't even 6 a.m., so I said no. Wouldn't you? I didn't want to hike for miles, climb a hill, then climb the mound itself, which wasn't nothing. It was more like a second hill stacked on top of the first one. Forget about it. Not until I've had some cups of tea.

Did I mention we were loud? That most of Europe was still sleeping?

Well, this man must have been an early riser himself, and must have heard our American racket, because as we passed his door he was standing there, waiting to invite us in for tea. He was on my side about it.

He set his kettle on a hot plate, spitted some bread on a bent wire hanger, waved it slowly over the gas-range flames, and there was toast. Extremely nice.

Here and Now

As for aesthetics, that's easy. Pick any good poem, and you're bound to find some. E.E. Cummings, for instance, gave us "mudluscious" and "puddlewonderful" for spring. Or there's Milton. This one's from *Paradise Lost*: When he needed a word that didn't exist yet, some way to make hell seem real on the page, he grabbed a prefix, a root, and a suffix and came up with "pandemonium." In "Vulture," Robinson Jeffers called the soul's ascension "enskyment." Of course! What else could the afterlife be when joined with those telescope eyes and that living wingspan?

And don't forget Anne Sexton. She's an alchemist. Start with "Hurry Up, Please, It's Time," especially the part where she's out in her backyard, celebrationally naked, saying, "Sun, you hammer of yellow, / you hat on fire, / you honeysuckle mama, / pour your blonde on me!" Absolutely. I suppose that this does stretch things a bit, though, since those aren't neologisms. Technically, they're epithets, but I really like hearing them: phrases she lines up like shots of tequila.

They're so much better than "Hit me on twitter," "Send your tweets to #hashtag whatever," and "Be sure to download the Free Coffee App @ whyamIdoingthis.com."

DOWN HERE ON THE COLD, COLD GROUND

With the New Year not so long ago, and in the spirit of resolutions, I plan to spend a minute each morning hating the guts of Vlad Sitnikov. He's the project leader of this startup called StartRocket, and what he wants to do is steal the night for himself and sell it for ad space.

This is true. A student at Utah Valley University (UVU) named Elijah Williams sent me a note with a link to an article in some magazine called *Futurism*. When I read it, I figured it was satire, like *The Onion*. Either that, or a hoax. Not according to Media Bias/Fact Check, though; I checked. *Futurism* is legit. So that means Vlad Sitnikov is real, and his words and rationalizations for sending up cube satellites to glow logos at all of us from space are real too. There's even a little *vimeo* to give us the idea: a logo in the way of the Aurora Borealis; another floating over Paris (the City of Lights, for God's sake); and that crappy KFC lettering in front of the stars above the Utah desert, over places like Capitol Reef that have been designated International Dark Sky Parks. Anyway, Vlad Sitnikov. You should hate him too.

About why he ought to get away with this, and with charging whichever corporations whatever gobs they'll pay, he said, "We are ruled by brands and events." He said, "The economy is the blood system of society. Entertainment and advertising are at its heart." All of which is wrong. I don't just mean unethical and empty; I mean incorrect.

People are the heart of society. We might put up with ads, or become numb to them, or get influenced or not, but if ads are the heart of society, then no amount of Peloton sweat and Geico harassment and Arby's creepiness and Verizon flunkies can ever defibrillate society back to life. "Corpsed" is all that is. "Corpsed"; I'm borrowing the expression from

Beckett's *Endgame*, a play about nihilism so brilliantly put together that you can't help feeling more alive, somehow affirmed, because there are people so good at making things—existential plays, books, dinners, lesson plans, fast-break alley-oops off the dribble, music (I'm looking at you, Tom Waits), chess moves, well-timed funny remarks—people so good at making things that you're glad you're alive just to notice them.

And people are the blood system too. The economy could be anything—goats, rum, some seashells—and has been; so the hell what? I'd rather have transactions of kindness. I'd rather bank on ethics, education, creativity. I'll value the purring of cats, and the possibility of seeing a mountain lion, and the way it smells in summer after it rains: almost new, but also dusty. I'll take all of those, plus memories, and the taste of just-picked peaches. They seem a lot more like lifeblood, at least to me. I mean, if the Renaissance were just a period of mercantile capitalism without literacy, cathedrals, and art, then who would care?

As for being "ruled by brands and events," I don't know what Sitnikov's talking about, although admittedly reading "This Startup Wants to Launch Giant Glowing Ads Into the Night Sky" (Jon Christian, *Futurism*, 8 Jan. 2019) has kept me busy writing this for hours. I guess you could say getting Elijah's email was an "event."

But here's the bigger story: It's been more than a few semesters since Elijah took my class, an Honors course called Modern Legacies. Our focus was "Futuristic Fiction: Paranoia or Prophecy?" As part of it, I asked students to bring in or email articles that seemed relevant to the ideas and warnings in works by Bradbury, Orwell, Wells, and Huxley, etc.—things they found that were interesting enough to share with me and with each other. Disturbing things, or heartening things, either way. The point was to connect our present time to either 1) dystopias, or 2) better alternatives with less pollution, less economic haves vs. have-nots, smarter food and energy production, smarter conservation and transportation, less T&A-driven shallowness, more wildness and wild animals, less veering toward demagogues and oligarchies, and all of them did. And some, like Elijah, have kept on doing it. Not because they're "ruled" but because they're interested. Sitnikov might call that the UVU "brand," but not me. To me, the language of business is like stepping in gum.

Not that there aren't brands that I like. I do. I like Häagen-Dazs. I get all my shoes from Fluevog's. If somebody asked, "You want a Foster's?" I'd say yes and drink that beer.

Maybe there'd be a stereo too, and a stack of CDs to look through. Maybe Camper Van Beethoven's *Key Lime Pie.*

And then Tom Waits singing "Cold Cold Ground."

MUSIC HISTORY

The first time I heard The Grateful Dead was on KOMO AM 1000, and I was hooked at age nine. It's an improbable origin story since KOMO was usually the source of Sonics games and the local news, but it's true.

More recently—today, in fact—The Dead were on satellite radio, a whole channel just for them. Am I the only one who didn't know this already? It's not the same thing as albums, but it's still pretty great.

What I like about The Dead isn't esoteric or anything. It's pretty plain. When you hear them, it sounds like they're just taking their instruments out for a walk. There's a breeze, but no serious wind, nothing that smacks of effort, just the sun and clouds working out the temperature together the way a kid works out which stick to float in the river next. What I mean is, they show us that music doesn't have to feel *worked on* to be *arrived at*.

And that's true of movies too. Take *Jaws* and *Jurassic Park*, for instance. Obviously, the animatronic T-Rex and raptors look more believable than the shark. It probably helps that the dinosaurs' electronics didn't have to work while submerged in the water. But the bigger point is that *Jurassic Park*, despite its advantage in mechanics, feels so made, so much like a movie, and *Jaws* doesn't, at least not to me. *Jaws* feels like we're there ourselves on Amity Island, or swimming in the ocean surrounding it, or on the piers in the harbor, or slopping chum from a bucket while we're rockingly seasick and breathing diesel fumes straight from the Orca's squeezebox engine. We're the people Quint keeps laughing at and then singing "You Fair Spanish Ladies." We're in the dining room with Hooper at the Brodys' house. We're the overwhelmed deputy holding up a hand-painted sign while the scene on the street is a crowd of greedy bozos blitzing the shelves in the bait shop. Nothing—and especially not when

Quint recounts the story of the USS *Indianapolis*—feels manufactured or difficult even though according to Spielberg, Scheider, Dreyfuss, and others—I've seen interviews—it was an ocean-sized strain of a movie to make. And I believe them. But it sure is easy to watch.

Same thing with teachers, and I've been lucky enough to have some good ones: Jim Taylor (Rogers High School) and Tom Campbell (Pacific Lutheran University, the PLU Lutes; short for Lutherans, although also that In-the-Beginning instrument given to us by Hermes when he scooped out a turtle, added frets and strings, and invented the bardic tradition).

What Mr. Taylor did was teach Advanced Placement English to teenagers, somehow revving us up about *Heart of Darkness* and J. Alfred Prufrock and writing character analyses, all without appearing to "teach." He didn't treat literature like a can you pry open and then dump out the can-shaped answers, and he didn't act scripted. No, it was more like Wallace Stevens' line in his most anthologized poem: "Let be be finale of seem." Mr. Taylor never had to *seem to* because he was *being it*.

And Professor Campbell was the same. How he taught Advanced Composition through the thunder-noise of McChord Air Force Base—it's practically next door to campus—I don't know, but he did it. Not easy, not easy at all, though he made it look that way.

I like poems that pull off this same kind of magic: Built Things that Seem as Unconstructed as a Forest. Take Anne Sexton; wow, can she do this. In "The Ambition Bird," to pick just one example, she hoists the Sistine Chapel, sends the Magi out on stage, yet still makes drinking cocoa the real stakes in her poem. "That warm brown mama," she calls it. Or take Richard Garcia, his poem "The Story of Keys." It's like The Grateful Dead meets origin story, meets the bow-legged grace of Charlie Chaplin. It's fantastic top to bottom, and then he ends it this way: "Anything can be a key: a piece of wire, / a safety pin, laughter."

It's perfect as is, I know, but to Garcia's list of anythings I'm going to add a lute. Hermes used his to entertain Zeus and con Apollo. And he did all this, if I remember correctly, on the day that he was born, which is some pretty genius work without looking like either.

My cat has that skill set, Anne Sexton had it, *Jaws* bit it in half and became it, and The Grateful Dead?—they went ahead and put it to music while seeming surprised that they knew what they were doing: *Oh, oh, and I wa-ant to kno-ow, how does the song go?* That's from "Uncle John's Band," bardic and elemental, a song like a sunlit river trading stories with the wind.

MUSIC HISTORY II

Two things happened that got me thinking. This was during the Get Lit! Literary Festival, and I was staying at the Red Lion at the Park, standing out back on one of the footbridges, listening to the Spokane River. Airports, hotel lobby, various conventioneers at various conventions, all in that fleecy-vest type of get-up, so maybe you can understand what happened: Out of the corner of my eye, I spotted a man walking up, pulling his rolling carry-on luggage. He stops to fidget, and I turn back to watch the river pouring through the open floodgates. Then I catch him again, crossing the bridge behind me, only he doesn't have a suitcase at all. He's walking his dog. He's holding a leash. Perception is crazy weird. Either the brain takes shortcuts, or it's trickable, or both. So that was the first thing.

The second is I'd gotten an email from my friend Jamie. He's the lead singer in a Steely Dan cover band in Seattle called Nearly Dan—good name—and I'd asked about his recent gigs, and he told me that performing is a blast but that he misses the way we used to play music back in college. Meaning, on an actual turntable. We even had a sort of duel going, one or the other of us leaving a record spinning and a note saying something like, "Drop the books, then the tone arm, and get your real education," or, "Try to beat this one, dumbass," and it would be a lesser-known track from Joni Mitchell's *Don Juan's Restless Daughters*, or "Dangerous Type" off *Candy-O* for a kick-back four-minute flashback since we'd grown up listening to The Cars. The exact record doesn't matter, and it isn't the point. The point is that cuing up music on the internet isn't the same. Jamie was saying that in his email, and I agree:

Pandora, the spawner of Spotify.

Pandora is the roller-wheeled suitcase rather than the actual dog. And as a name, it's pretty lame and upside down because whoever made it up was skipping the facts: Pandora's Box wasn't a good thing, not unless you want blight to fly out and everything nice to be lost except for hope. Tactile connection?—gone. Design and aesthetics?—*whoosh*. Intention, progress, and resolution?—voided out in favor of disconnected singles, then some other ones like synonyms, and so on. She shouldn't have her name misused that way, especially not after the mythological whammy the Ancient Greeks gave her in the first place, the same bad rap as Eve: "Don't open that box, and don't touch that fruit tree. Just sit there and die of curiosity." Followed by: "Well, thanks to you two, everyone's going to have allergies now. And zits and mucous and cancer. They'll all stink, and struggle, and women will yell their guts out in childbirth, and people will be cursed with mosquitos and TV commercials and then robbed of their autonomy in old age. All because of you." That's a suck-ass story if you think about it, but I'll still take that original Tragedy over today's new Whatever-You-Call-It, with software doing your choosing for you based on stuff that you already know you like. Maybe if it sparked curiosity, or if Spotify did, or the next thing comin' 'round the mountain, but nope; they just replace our curiosity with I-Don't-Know.

Q: What's in the box?
A: Just more boxes.
Q: Can I have a bite of your apple?
A: If I can have a bite of yours.

There used to be whole albums, these constructed sonic worlds, arranged in order and jacketed with cover art and liner notes. And some-times those liner notes were like anthropological essays, or like eulogies for gone-away eras. Check out The Violent Femmes, for example: *Add It Up (1981–1993)*. Or Nat Hentoff and others on jazz recordings. Reading the liner notes on Charles Mingus' *Mingus Ah Um* (Columbia 1959) is how I was reminded about what an opportunistic, race-baiting creep Governor

Orval Faubus was. If his name's not familiar, you can Wiki him, but I'd rather have "Fables of Faubus" spinning while I read from a record jacket I can hold in my hands. If I have to remember Faubus at all, or notice similarities between him and politicos these days ("Pandora, find me a present-day Orval-Eugene-type; bingo, out pops somebody yelling about Mexicans, Muslims, and women who weren't in his beauty pageants), then doing it via keystrokes or swiping would only make it worse.

But getting back to music—I bet you could tell Siri to sing Duran Duran's "Hungry Like The Wolf" and get something that sounds like an existentially sad Chihuahua, or say, "Alexa, play 'Miles From Nowhere' by Cat Stevens," and no doubt the song will play, but it's not the same as lowering the tone arm, or opening the CD case and then the tray. . .

From that place on the footbridge over the Spokane River, you can see the dam, the open floodgates, colossal water pouring through and climbing the concrete banks of the channel, and it's pretty good, but it isn't my favorite spot. The river is the least itself there and more like *somebody else's*. It isn't a whole album, just a packaged single. On repeat,

repeat,

repeat,

repeat,

repeat.

TWO CURES FOR BILLBOARDS

In the Blue Mountains up in Oregon, they don't mess around. It's different than eastern Washington, where I thought I'd seen a sign for "Ultimatum Ridge." Only I didn't; it was one of those eye-skip things. Southbound on I-82, winding into Yakima County, what you really see is a sign for Umtanum Ridge.

Which is fine, of course, and not nearly as lightweight as my own state of Utah—Sandy, Park City, Pleasant Grove, and a town, no kidding, called Bountiful.

Not so in Oregon. True, they have LaGrande (rhymes with "the hand"), but before you twist down to town through the mountains, you'll pass signs along the way for Deadman Pass, Poverty Flat Road, Old Emigrant Hill Road, and even something called Steer's Bones. A gulch, a canyon, an avalanche dance club? I don't know, but it sure isn't Bountiful.

Even better, there are signs that say, "Max Fine for Littering $6,520." Holy cow. *Holy steer's bones!* And now I want that fine in Utah too, and also to redefine "litter" since to me the biggest form of it is billboards. I don't care if they're the old-school kind or those glowing grids of pixels; they need to go. Take all of that garbage down. Restore our sight lines to the Wasatch Mountains. Thousands of square feet of sky reappearing overnight, and no more rectangular shadows. Take them all down, make a stack, and call it Poverty Flats. As in, these things cheapen what it means to be gifted with eyes.

There's no way the hawks will miss billboards. And somehow we'll still find hamburgers. And if $6,520 seems too high for a fine, "Too bad," I'll tell our legislature. "Would you rather have miles of nudity? Because my other plan is that billboards will have to go nude."

I don't mean photos of naked people; I just mean the word: "Sleep Inn Nudity," "Truck Stop Nudity," "Timpanogos Regional Hospital—Not Bigger. Just Better Nudity," "Cabela's Outdoor Nudity Gear," "Bank of America Nudity Checking," and so on. . . "Make America Nude Again."

That should spur the Utah crowds to pull them down if nothing else will. First, an inhale of shock, and then some well-deserved destruction.

You could hear it from Salt Lake City to Ultimatum Ridge.

METEOROLOGY

There's a writer, Brady Udall, I figure a ton of people already love or at least have heard about. He's good. He's from out West here—northern Arizona, southern Utah—and in his first book, *Letting Loose the Hounds*, there's a story called "Vernon" I won't go into very much except to tell you about one detail: this dead guy's giant woodpile. It's enormous. Almost Cascade-Mountain-sized. Anyway, it's hard to overlook, and yet it disappears into the background of the larger story about three 21-year-old friends. A story's landscape can do that, fade away a little, since it's the characters' actions or inactions that tend to interest us the most.

The thing is, though, this woodpile is more than a part of the setting. Yes, it's a hang-out spot for them, a vantage point from which to see their town, the pine woods, the surrounding mountains, and maybe even the sheriff's wife (we're told she's got quite a body) who is rumored to do her yard work in the nude. And yes, it's there to give the narrator a chance to imagine epic endings—lighting a fire so big that you can see it from Mars, or maybe making a misstep so the three of them get avalanched—but it's also a symbol calling out, "Less ant, more grasshopper." Why split and pile up so much wood you can't burn it all in one lifetime? And remember the guy who did this is already dead.

Literature, from *Gather ye rosebuds* to *Waiting for Godot*, is full of this same story. It doesn't wear out. How come? Because we don't listen.

Though that's too simple, of course. Take Sam: He's an Honors student, and he also has some important job as a liaison on campus. He's wearing a suit and tie and a backpack when I see him. We say, "Hey," and I ask, "How's it going?" and he says, "Fine. Just looking for a hole to crawl into for a couple hours to study." Good for him. What am I doing? I'm walking around, taking a break in the middle of writing this. Good for me. I'm the point guard of the Grasshoppers, at least for now.

And it's not as if I'm un-conflicted about it. I've got drafts of freshman essays all over my desk that aren't going to fix themselves. I got one—one!—done before I moved them aside and started writing this instead.

I also don't own an umbrella. There isn't much point in Utah. I had one once in the old days in Tacoma, but it broke—sideways March winds about 40 miles an hour; 40-degree rain blasts, driven and determined; umbrellas held shoulder high like nylon shields until they flipped, inverted, turned inside-out and rib-snapped. I never replaced it. It rained, and I got wet, like this was a deal we'd worked out together, a deal that suited the rain and me just fine. . .

I don't know enough about neurons to explain it, but thinking of the rain just now reminds me of The Day of the Quail. They took over the neighborhood. There must have been 80—I finally stopped counting, that's how many—going by in this surprising line, a group of grown-ups leading the way, then dozens of these jellybean chicks skittering along behind, right down the middle of my street, then left around the corner. I would have liked it even more if there'd been rain to go along with this—*Ah-ha*, that's the connection—but never mind. It was cool.

I told my neighbor Mike about it a couple minutes later, and he took off and started knocking on doors, gathered a group to go catch up and see them. He even stopped traffic on 900 East so all those quail could get safely to the park. He likes birds. And everyone was happy. They were glad that they'd stopped whatever they were doing, glad that they'd slowed down.

You know who wasn't, who didn't want to?—the people in cars.

Or maybe their cars were in charge of the driving, and the cars didn't think there was time to pull over, cut their engines for a while, and have a look.

ZOOLOGY

My neighbor Mike has added an extra ecosystem to his yard. Nothing elaborate, just a daily pile of birdseed next to some groundcover bushes and vines, but it brings all sorts of birds around, and mice too. And other animals up the food chain.

One morning, for instance, when my son Jameson was four, he asked from behind me in his car seat, "What is that?" And when I couldn't find it, "In our little tree."

We'd just pulled up to the curb out front—no snow on the ground yet, so this must have been November—and there it was: a hawk, exactly bark colored, improbably big for the branch it was perched on, eight feet away from the sparrow zone, waiting. And we waited too.

Another time it was my cat next door, as tensed and patient as a spring-loaded sphinx, his eyes trained just beyond the birdseed on those vines. He knew there were mice there.

There's another story that's sort of like this and sort of not. It has to do with a sea lion up in Seattle—very smart or very lazy, depending on your attitude; resourceful or greedy, take your pick. He was camping out at the Ballard Locks, right in front of the fish ladder since to get from Puget Sound back to Lake Washington and then on again to their spawning rivers, the salmon needed a way to climb around. Park your blubber, open your mouth, and they practically swim right in. They finally put him on a cargo plane, flew him all the way to Baja, and he swam right back.

I can't help wishing that poetry did that too, incited that same sort of patience and pilgrimage. An open book like a fish ladder. Images like birdseed. People all spring-coiled and waiting, ready for something to step out from the greenery, maybe a haiku—

Hate is a shovel,
love is a river. Both dig.
But one just digs holes—

or a sonnet, or even a simple blessing: "May your talons and foreclaws and spirits be sharp. May you find your way back from the Baja coast to eat a hundred poems."

MARINE BIOLOGY

As a kid growing up in Washington, I had a giant admiration for Slick Watts. "Downtown" Freddie Brown too, of course, swishing rainbow jumpers from deep. If they'd had the three-point line back then, forget about it; you would've needed a pinball machine to keep score.

Slick Watts was first, though. Slick Watts of the Seattle SuperSonics: bald in a league full of afros or longish hair. He wore a headband when nobody else did. He invented the scoop shot! And if I'm misremembering—if others deployed it too—then I don't want to know. Slick Watts ruled, and I used to imitate him while going against invisible defenders in my driveway.

But if you're betting that I liked the Seahawks too, you lose. *Nunca. Nada.* By the time the NFL added Tampa Bay and Seattle, I was already a wild-thing Raiders' fan. I used to run through other kids' arm tackles, thinking (maybe even chanting aloud) "Mark van Eeghen, Mark van Eeghen." I watched Kenny Stabler's 1974 miracle pass to Clarence Davis, knocking the Dolphins from the playoffs; what a happiness launch pad! And I saw Rob Lytle fumble in front of the goal line, saw the Raiders recover, saw the referees conspire to give the Denver Broncos the ball back and a free pass to Super Bowl XII, which they lost, karmically, 27 to 10. Anyway, sports; I'm saying I liked them a bit. So when it came time to write a report on a famous person's biography, who do you think I picked?

Jacques Cousteau. The ocean's own Messenger Angel.

Before him, everyone who wanted to explore underwater had to do it like Captain Nemo, wearing that lead-boots/air-hose contraption dreamt up by—no kidding—Leonardo da Vinci; that's how dated the design was.

Well, Jacques Cousteau wanted to swim not trundle, so he went to work inventing scuba gear: "self-contained underwater breathing apparatus." The fact that he used English for the acronym is just further proof that he knew what he was doing. Americans had all the televisions. It was mainly to kids like me that he was bringing the Good News. I'm saying, when I grew up I wanted to play in the NFL or NBA, but I wanted to *be* Jacques Cousteau.

I planned on majoring in Marine Biology, but it didn't work out that way. Instead, I went with literature and writing, and I can't say I regret it. A lot of the time, though, I find myself writing about sharks; or the coastline, seagulls, coral reefs, humpbacks, manta rays, salmon, and waves. Jungians and astrologers could probably offer reasons, even interesting ones that I might be glad to hear. A mermaid could offer her take on it, saying some are just more spell-cast than others. I don't know. Love isn't easy to quantify. It's easier just to praise it, so why not?

STANDING AT HALF MOON BAY STATE BEACH, FACING WEST: A SHARK SONG
I like how they live, the way they hunt sea lions,
the way they attack those meat loaves

when they flop in off the rocks.
What glorious feeding:

the silent, giant hunger underwater
with its blank eyes, gallery of teeth,

its jaws thrown forward, impossibly wide,
then down with dispassion, thrashing its catch—

a bloody avalanche—
ripping out a hundred pounds each bite,

returning through clouds of torn blubber for more,
the dorsal fin cutting like a scythe. . .

what glorious food: seals full of salmon
full of grunion spiced with krill.

I remember Thanksgiving at a rich friend's home,
having goose stuffed with duck stuffed with quail,

all seasoned with tangerine blossoms and cloves,
basted in whiskey,

served with a sauce from currants and plums.
It's got to be heaven tearing in,

it must be god-like
to survive a million years, to be perfected:

Devourer of Ocean Life, Terror to Man,
absolutely unmoved by and worthy of our praise.

May they outlast us.
May the seas swim with good things to eat.

RACCOON VERSES

There Used to Be a Time When Foxes Were Brown
In the Old Songs about Washington, a raccoon and fox
had an argument, each one bragging that he was the better thief.

The fox stole some colors from the sunset
and painted, for himself, the first flowers,

but the raccoon grabbed their pollen
and gave it to bees to carry everywhere.

The fox got mad.
And more bold.

He picked the lock and entered
the Land of the Dead: endless bones to gnaw on.

Quiet as a current, the raccoon followed.
Quickly, while the fox was eating, he took and hid the door,

and in the Old Songs, this was good;
it meant the living and dead could now speak.

The fox saw one last chance to even the score:
He poked a paw into Thunder's pocket,

trying to swipe a streak of lightning,
and the flash,

if you listen to the Old Songs,
burned his fur the colors of smoke and fire.

That's an origin story about the color of foxes, so the raccoon's just a minor character. He isn't even the antagonist since the fox is really his own worst problem. But the minor character is the one on my mind because the other morning I saw a baby raccoon and was glad that I did. So were Jen and Quentin and Jameson. And so were our neighbors who kept a kind of casual vigil while he slept all day and evening in their tree.

He'd been moving around under their groundcover vines in this spot where cats like to hide and ambush birds, so I figured he was just a cat until he strolled out onto the grass: this baby raccoon.

I got my boys to come and look, but by then he'd gone up the tree, walking up the branches the way that you and I would walk down the sidewalk. And that's where he was, still napping, when my wife Jen got home in the afternoon.

If he were a bird, so what? But he wasn't. He was rare. And I think that's what a poem is too: this unexpected creature stepping out from under our language and climbing up a tree. And you there to notice.

I like that definition: Poems are raccoons. I like it for two reasons; first, because it's easy to remember, and second because it doesn't make sense unless you're thinking in metaphor and imagery. I'll bet that's how William Carlos Williams felt after he'd written his famous wheelbarrow poem. I mean, I don't know for sure, but it doesn't seem impossible since a poem is a well-made language contraption, and if you're willing to pay attention, then it can take our daily crap-loads and roll them away.

I'm going to try to imitate that same kind of balance now and circle back to foxes and raccoons:

WHY THE RACCOON'S TAIL HAS STRIPES

A fox is a fox—bright zigzag, cunning stomach—
but who is Raccoon,

which way do his whiskers point?
You can knock all day on that question; nobody's home,

just a key beneath the welcome mat,
and inside, hanging from his ceiling,

strange chandeliers:
arrangements of keys and hoop earrings,

loose change forever going missing,
the silver promises of corkscrews, laughter,

desire. . . anything shiny.
All those years spent collecting—here they are.

He isn't a thief; he just looks like a bandit.
Take back whatever you like.

He knows his tail is a lesson in perspective:
Find it/Lose it, Have it/Vanish, making stripes.

COMMONPLACE BEASTS AND WHERE TO FIND THEM

My Front Yard
I have a squirrel. Not a pet, a visitor. That's important. It makes a difference. He started coming around last year, with his six movements-and-still-nesses per second, hanging around with the birds at the feeder, his cheeks like pictures of Dizzy Gillespie. And this year he's back.

I wasn't sure he would be because in January I'd seen a dead squirrel in the road—run over on 900 East, a few leaps from Fairmont Park—and thought it might be him.

But it wasn't. He showed up again in April, zigzagging over to the porch steps, then backflip-sprinting to the tree trunk to execute a perfect leap-cling maneuver. Then he jumped down to break the pogo speed record, then sat in the grass, his tail like a question mark, watching while I went to get the mail, like I was the interesting one,

The Floor of My Living Room
but I wasn't. I can't move like that. I can barely even describe it, and espe-cially not now, because my cat keeps using my pen as a chin scratcher, and he's licking my arm to help groom me. He's shedding a Maine Coon fur-storm in advance of the coming heat wave, so he probably figures that I should be doing that too.

And now his paws and head are on my forearm, which he's holding down and using as a pillow, and my lack of total stillness is earning me a stare.

I can see his point, and I'm trying to write without moving. But just like I can't go face first down a tree trunk, I can't use a pen without moving at least a little bit.

Herman Franks Ballpark, Salt Lake City
A while back the coaches threw an End-of-the-Season Party for the little leaguers: burgers, a few contests, a few raffles, and an Iron Man piñata.

For Jameson, the piñata was the highlight, but it turns out I liked it too because when the bat finally blasted it open and all the eight-year-olds became a scramble-crouch of grabbing, Jameson just tracked the head flying off and picked that up instead: packed full of candy and easy to carry. Pretty smart.

In the ecosystem of childhood, it was like a sudden evolution.

Parkland, Washington
I saw a squirrel pull a similar trick one summer when I was still a student at PLU (Pacific Lutheran University). This was in front of the library, just off the quad—the grass part with all the cedar trees, not the red brick plaza in front of Eastvold Hall.

A girl was sitting on a bench, having lunch (a bag of McDonald's, a strawberry shake) and feeding her fries to a squirrel.

She'd toss one. He'd eat it.

She'd toss another, and so on, until the squirrel was close enough to take them from her hand.

Then she turned away to get another, and that's when the squirrel made off with her shake, clutching and running like a leapfrog, a bounding miracle, straight for a tree, and her coming after: *"Hey!"*

The trunk is what stumped him. He wound up dropping the cup while scaling it, which is how I know the shake was strawberry. All this neon pink *splopped* out on the ground.

On the TV News
Even without the sound on, you can tell the politicos are lying. Impossible to look that smug without lying first to themselves.

Tonight and Tomorrow
My cat is already sleeping again, and I'd rather be up instead of lying here.

But he's 108 now in human years, and limping from what seems like hip pain, and he won't drink water for the last two days, so I'm sticking nearby for quiet company.

My smell is a smell he's known forever. And his ears twitch slightly from the sound of pen on paper. And I'm glad my squirrel wasn't the one run over.

But in the morning I hope my cat goes out and stalks him from the mailbox to the moon.

WHY WE HAVE BIRDS

Salt Lake City

Watson's favorite hangout spot is at the foot of the bird bath in our neighbor's yard. Or sometimes he'll perch on the edge like a gargoyle. Sometimes he'll take a drink himself. The coloring on his face is slightly crooked, and his right eye is kind of cross-eyed, which makes him look like. . . well, let's just call it "not too deep a thinker." But he's worked it out: Birds keep landing there, and Watson loves to stalk birds.

One time he actually caught one, a dove. Compared to his little cat face, it looked as big as a pelican. And Watson's way of walking back with it—tail high, stepping through the iris leaves—was almost stately, like a drum major leading his own parade. Plus, somehow despite all the flapping and the size of the cargo in his mouth, he seemed to be grinning.

[Brief Pause]

This might make some readers mad, I know—that we let our son's cats go outside. I hope not. That isn't my intention. But still, I need to address the cat question—

First, I admit to being pissed off when people's dogs came after my cat Gruden (May 18, 2002 to June 17, 2020). A couple times, I even had to jump in, and both of us—I could tell from his expression—thought it sucked that he'd gotten too old to fight back. I thought, *There shouldn't be dogs, and people out walking them, letting them mess with my cat in his own damn yard!* But then I had to admit that dogs are dogs, and it doesn't mean their owners are terrible. What I'm saying, I guess, is that things can get pretty tangled. Should we *never* let our son's cats go outside because *maybe* they'll kill a bird? I'm willing to admit that I'm not sure.

But second, admitting that I'm not sure about this isn't true of every-
one, and there are numbers—seemingly improbable ones—to back up
those with more certainty than me. Here's what I mean: According to the
American Bird Conservancy, cats kill 2.4 billion birds each year (although
obviously not the herons, geese, and other birds I'll be talking about
in a minute). The estimated number of house cats in the U.S. is right
around 59 million, and many of them are too old to catch birds, or they're
indoor cats, or they've been declawed, which seems awful, but sometimes
people do that. Anyway, to get to that number—2.4 billion total—then
every single house cat in America would have to catch and kill 40.7 birds
per year. Not the *one* dove Watson caught but 39 more. And does he?
Absolutely not.

So does this mean that the information from the American Bird
Conservancy is incorrect, possibly even alarmist? That's not what I'm
saying. And I'm not going to hold their own statement that 69 percent
of these bird deaths are caused by *un-owned* cats against them. I'm just
saying that to keep an animal stuck inside when it wants to be outside
means weighing one animal's instincts, preference, and sense of self and
joy against another's. We make choices, and the choice I've made is cats.
I don't choose dogs, but I try to forgive them. And I've chosen the side of
my neighbor Mike who's on the side of hawks.

Mike's not a scientist, but he's also not unreasonable, and he knows
where the neighborhood owl lives and isn't bored when I tell him what
the quail have been up to. Mike keeps wishing (me too) that the hawks
would feed on these Eurasian collared doves, only they don't. They don't
for some reason that the hawks aren't telling. So when I mentioned that
Watson had caught one, he said, "Good. Now he needs to catch some
more because they're crowding out the native doves." This isn't incon-
sequential, and there's actually some logic here: Hawks like to eat our
mourning doves, and these Eurasian doves are territorial, so having them
take over our yards means fewer meals for hawks.

Am I being anecdotal? I suppose so. And perhaps this debate is unwinnable. But it wasn't really my intention to win. My intention was to talk about birds, and mostly the larger ones. Drought is in the news again, the same as every summer, so I've been thinking about our water, and wetlands, and also some other things too.

Tracy Aviary, Salt Lake City
I didn't know peacocks could fly, did you? But they can. Or else they're good climbers. Because up in the tree limbs, fifty feet above, we saw this waterfall curtain of feathers, peacock blue.

Hwy 40, East of Heber
I remembered about that peacock while driving up to Strawberry Reservoir, maybe because Watson had climbed up a tree before we left, and I forgot to help him down first.

Oh no, I thought, about sixty miles later. *What if he's stuck? What if he's still up there, sad that he couldn't catch the finch, and sad that he's thirsty?*

My Best Friend Jay
When we were kids, his parents called him Jaybird. And that's what Jen and I call our son Jameson too. So does his niece. Every time she sees him. And then again some more across the dinner table: *Hi Jaybird, Hi Jaybird.* He's got a huge fan.

He's also got a smartphone, like the rest of his generation—those gizmos forever with them like a third opposable thumb. Jen says all his proclamations are just what kids do when they get to this age. We'll say, "How do you know that?" or "Where did you hear that?" or "I'm pretty sure that isn't right" and get back a grumpier answer than we wanted to hear. But I *did* like this one: Coming down the stairs one day, Jameson said, "Hey, Dad, did you know that crows are the smartest kind of bird? They're part of the kroners, or carbonites, or, anyway, some kind of family."

"You mean corvids?"

"Yeah, corvids. So are blue jays. Whenever blue jays see people, they criticize what they're doing and like to yell at them." He said this with one of those smiles, you know, like he didn't mean to let it show but it halfway slipped out.

"Where'd you hear that?" I asked.

"Nowhere," he said. "I've just known it for a while now."

"So it's lucky we've always called you Jaybird."

"Yes it is."

All the Western U.S. and Then Some

Everyone paying attention knows the West is in serious trouble. Australia too. A whole planetary roll call of places: wildfires, record heat waves, fill-in-the-blank drought—*mega, decades-long, state-of-emergency, extreme;* any of those adjectives will do. And the heat? A hundred million mussels baked right there and reeking in the tide pools.

And inland isn't any better. No, each river, each body of water, is setting new records for lowness every year. I'm not an ornithologist, but I still know how to ask: If moored boats are practically dry-docked in their slips, then what does that mean for all the migratory birds depending on the wetlands? Picture it like this: You're trying to drive across the country—say, from Phoenix to Billings to Seattle to Alaska—and then back home, only you can't, not really, because these geese have bulldozed every rest stop, and some egrets have blown up all the gas stations, and even the monarch butterflies are getting in on the action, raining down poison on the off-ramp restaurants then setting the next-to-last grocery store on fire.

So anyway, trouble.

That Saying from the Coal Mines

They used to take canaries down with them, living alarm bells. If the bird died, then *Get the hell outta here!. . .* Well?

You could say blue mussels aren't the same, I guess. But their shells fold open like wings.

Later That Day, Home from Strawberry

Watson was fine; don't worry. And Sherlock—that's our other cat—he was fine too. The rescue place told us, "They're a bonded pair," and they were right; they're totally friends, stampeding down the staircase together, then sliding into the turn like speed skaters mixed with Wile E. Coyote, or else napping in a yin-yang symbol since they're white-and-gray and black-and-white.

Up at the reservoir, there was a heron on the dock. Its shape, all its movements: calligraphy. Two pelicans. A seagull. Even cranes, or at least I think so. They were too far away from the boat to be sure, a dozen white blurs along the shoreline.

My son Quentin said, "I guess I missed the cranes. I wish I'd seen them."

"Next time, " I said. "There'll be other days."

I hope that's true.

THREE SKIES

Herons
The first time I saw a Great Blue Heron, I was six. In the morning when I went out to play, it was in our backyard.

We had sort of a wetland back there, with frogs and cattails and everything. Turns out a water main was leaking underground, had been leaking for years, but the heron wouldn't have cared about the reason. It probably just saw our marsh while flying by and decided to glide on down to do its one-leg standing, to hold still as a cattail 'til a frog came by, then stab with its harpoon beak. As if somehow a piece of the sky had come alive and was paying me a visit.

Owls
Sometimes I wonder what the Answer People think about. Probably not a lot. Say a question comes up—*Mosquito*—they just smack it with their answer. Or a new encounter comes along, and the new thing is wrong because it doesn't fit their answer. To me, that seems like a pretty dull life, and I like questions more. I don't mean questions like, "How do you spell 'vacuum cleaner'?" or, "How do you pronounce 'Qatar'?" I mean questions there might not be an answer for. I mean questions that take your mind on a walk and keep you company whichever way you go:

THE CHURCH OF THE STARS AND THE MOON
Of course they weren't resurrecting. But the mouse I found in the garden one evening (dropped by the carrots when my cat got bored), and the dead bird, broken, in the deck chair (such a nice spot to stretch out easy while you're thinking, while you're pinning one wing and watching the

other one flail), in the morning, when I went back to toss them, they were gone. And then I could hear it for certain: a call that wasn't like *Hooo* but more like *More-more*.

And so I had an owl, a little piece of neighborhood lightning. I'd swing by the pet store, buy mice to stock the yard, and keep watch, my eyes tuned to shadows. I'd will the street to sit still and be quiet so the owl would let go and glide, carve its arc across the backyard darkness, just a hitch—one moment—when the talons clutched, then gone, the best part of summer.

I only saw it once.

But I found where the bones wound up: always at the base of a telephone pole in the alley behind the garage. I noticed ants one day in their organized scramble—sure enough: an above-ground catacomb, a toss of miniature driftwood, deposit of *dead*.

It probably liked the crossbeam (like a long, high table with an open view of below) and ate unhurried, and ate well, then sat like a messenger angel in The Church of the Stars and the Moon. Don't believe it's impossible. If angels are real, then an angel might be an owl.

They do seem to be intercessors, calling out across the empty spaces, their gold eyes filling up zeroes, their wings like a bridge, something reaching from up to down, lower to higher, at least for a while.

I miss my owl's company. I wish it had stayed all summer.

But maybe, like angels, they belong to no one. Maybe wildness is an answer from the sky.

Kites

I've heard a lot of people say they want a perfect life, which makes sense, and who doesn't?. . . until you think about it. When you think about it, doesn't that sound a bit greedy?

Yogi Berra had a great quote about this. He was a catcher for the New York Yankees, and you've probably heard of him. He was famous for saying all these accidentally genius-goofball things. Ever heard, "It's déjà vu all over again"? That was him.

This one is better, though. He said, "If life was perfect, it wouldn't be."

And the author Kurt Vonnegut proved it. He wrote three stories titled "Harrison Bergeron," "The Euphio Question," and "Tomorrow and Tomorrow and Tomorrow." They're funny-smart and dystopian. In the first, we finally have equality. In the second, happiness comes with an on-switch. And in the third, there's a medicine called "anti-gerasol" so that people stop aging and can live forever. Which sounds about perfect, right?—everyone's equal, everyone's happy, and nobody dies. But if life was perfect, it wouldn't be, and Vonnegut shows us the truth of this in a couple dozen pages.

Still, we don't have to get gloomy about it, or afraid, or so worried that we're going to fail at something that we never even start. Life is a good time to try a few things. If it leads to perfection, even once, then that's a bonus. But trying is first:

THE MAN HAS A HEART LIKE A KITE,
and he knows it, knows it's a bad idea.
For one thing, the wind keeps pushing him around,

wheeling him in spirals,
lifting him halfway to Venus,

then watching him drop.
He's sick of crash landings, fed up

with hanging upside down in trees—
a mouth full of feathers and twigs in his nose.

But don't ask what I think; I'm the same way.
I won't advise him to grab more gravity,

won't offer him bowls of stone soup;
what good is a kite in the garage?

Suppose he breaks his neck next time, so what?
No one's impressed by caution,

or sprawls on the couch, reading books about it,
or goes to the park with a rock on the end of a string.

TAKE THE A) SEX QUIZ, B) PERSONALITY TEST, OR C) QUICK BREAK FROM BUSYWORK

1. Would you rather be a cheetah or an antelope?
2. Would you rather be an orca or a wolf?
3. If you answered cheetah and orca, go to 4; if cheetah and wolf, proceed to 6. If you answered antelope with either, skip to 23, one for each hour you'll be running. That's the trade-off for looking delicious. . . that, and a diet of grasses, or maybe iris bulbs if you're fortunate and the rains have done your digging for you since your ungulate hooves aren't famous for scooping dirt.
4. Congratulations, you're amphibious, fast in both Africa and ocean.
5. But you lack the resonance of wolfsong and whalesong. Someone's got a sexier voice.
6. Congratulations, you're a miracle, capable of high-speed, hairpin turning combined with the stamina to hunt for forty miles. You're canine and feline, Northern Hemisphere and Southern, night and day. But also fractured. A wild rift, a howling schism, and
7. perfect as scissors, I agree, but
8. the world isn't paper, it's rock.
9. And you orcas, I haven't forgotten you. I see you raising your dorsal fins. I can hear you thinking *There's nothing wrong with my voice. My squeaks are expressive, and I run my meetings efficiently.* Go to 10.
10. Certainty's less creative than doubt. It puts clock hands on every circle.
11. But doubt is what rounds some circles into spheres. It's what taught us that we don't fall off.
12. You're darn right that's a paradox.

13. Doubt is the catch then rising in the wolf's song, after which longing seems longer. . .

14. When will it come, our best moment? When will it come, that feeling we're imagining?

15. Let's turn our attention to fruit now: Would you rather have cherries or watermelon?

16. Good questions. I'll answer them one at a time.

17. Yes, the watermelon's real, not seedless.

18. Yes, the cherries are Rainiers.

19. The watermelon's 19¢-a-lb. You can slice it however you want to.

20. The cherries come from a roadside stand. It's hot, but it isn't breezeless.

21. If you answered cherries, go to 25. You get an extra hour for just enjoying.

22. If you answered watermelon, good for you, although any fruit would be perfect. Except bananas. That's where we draw the line, and I know a dog who'd back me up on that—Dennis and Gloria Martin's springer spaniel, Pacific Lutheran University, some dozen or more of us invited over, food laid out on the table, wine and whiskey. And Edith Piaf on the stereo, reinventing singing. And their dog enjoying the party—so many hands, so willingly reaching things for her: grapes, and carrots, and baba ghanouj; sourdough rolls, and smoked salmon; turkey wrapped around Irish cheddar; and marzipan tartlets, and blackberry pie, and everything good. Except bananas. Bananas were a definite *Nope*, which reminds me,

23. I didn't pick antelope, you did. You chose *Gravity-defying Rangeland Lightning*. But along with that comes restlessness and troubled sleep.

24. Now think of your favorite sexual position. Go ahead, this quiz can wait for a minute. . . Is the person you're picturing doing this with more Orca, Wolf, or Cherries; more Gravity-Defying or Hairpin Turn; or All of the Above?

25. I think our work here is almost done. A final question ought to wrap it:

26. If you could do one thing a second time, what would it be?

ACKNOWLEDGMENTS

Thank you to Simmons Buntin, Editor-in-Chief of *Terrain.org*, where earlier versions of these essays, sometimes under different titles, first appeared between 2015 and 2024.

"Addition + Subtraction" was accepted for production in an evening of monologues called *The Strand Project 2017*, a theatrical collaboration between Selah Dinner Theater and Lit Youngstown, with performances on June 2-3 and June 9-10, 2017, in Struthers, OH.

"Poetry" and "Raccoon Verses" appeared as Parts 1 and 2 of "A Field Guide to Poems in Three Parts" in the book *Far Villages: Welcome Essays for New and Beginner Poets*, Abayomi Animashaun, editor (New York: Black Lawrence Press, 2020).

"In the Beginning Was a River" and "Music History II" appeared as sections 1 and 6 of "Seven Rivers" in *Tales from the River*, Donna Mulvenna and Margi Prideaux, editors (Parndana, South Australia: Stormbird Press, 2018).

"Addition + Subtraction" appeared in *Awake in the World: Riverfeet Anthology*, Daniel J. Rice, editor (Bemidji, MN and Livingston, MT: Riverfeet Press, 2017).

"Environmental Studies" and "In the Beginning Was a River" were reprinted by *The Dark Mountain Project* online, Nick Hunt, editor (29 Aug. 2018).

"In the Beginning Was a River" was reprinted online in *About Place Journal: Dignity as an Endangered Species in the 21st Century*, Pam Uschuk, editor (1 May 2019).

Wakefield Press is an independent publishing and
distribution company based in Adelaide, South Australia.
We love good stories and publish beautiful books.
To see our full range of books, please visit our website at
www.wakefieldpress.com.au
where all titles are available for purchase.
To keep up with our latest releases and news,
subscribe to the *Wakefield Weekly* at
https://mailchi.mp/wakefieldpress/subscribe

Find us!

Facebook: www.facebook.com/wakefield.press
Instagram: www.instagram.com/wakefieldpress

www.ingramcontent.com/pod-product-compliance
Lightning Source LLC
Chambersburg PA
CBHW020020030726
47499CB00007B/2192